To receive more than $2,500 in FREE BONUSES from leading Network Marketing experts and trainers (like Dr. Joe Rubino, Tom "Big Al" Schreiter, John Terhune, and many others), please follow the simple three steps below. These FREE bonuses are intended to support the success of all network marketers in any company.

1. Purchase your copy of *15 Secrets Every Network Marketer Must Know* by Dr. Joe Rubino and John Terhune.
2. Visit http://www.cprsuccess.com/15secrets and enter the number on your receipt proving your purchase.
3. You will receive in response an e-mail with complete instructions on how to claim your FREE BONUSES with no further obligation.

This is our way of thanking you for your purchase and for making a commitment to your Network Marketing Success!

D0052863

"Both new and experienced network marketers and their organizations can profit both personally and professionally from the informational wealth shared by these network marketing masterminds."
— Stacy Ann Henderson, Editor-in-Chief,
Home Business® Magazine, www.homebusinessmag.com

"*15 Secrets Every Network Marketer Must Know* transcends other MLM "How To . . ." books. In this powerful, flowing text, Rubino and Terhune meld the essence of being a leader along with the knowledge of exactly what causes attraction and enrollment success. These two talents united create an alchemy of wisdom — concepts that every networker really must know."
— Randy Anderson, Author of
High Performance Networking

"*15 Secrets Every Network Marketer Must Know* is a thorough course in book format that will support any network marketer to acquire the most essential business building principles necessary to lay a solid foundation for success and accomplishment. Rubino and Terhune combine to share 15 critical distinctions that will cause your team to soar."
— Dr. Tom Ventullo, President,
TheCenterForPersonalReinvention.com

"You don't have to be in network marketing to profit by this book . . . but if you are, you hold in your hands the best yet."
— Charles T. Jones, Author of *Life Is Tremendous*

"Over the past 10 years I have had the pleasure of working alongside both Dr. Joe Rubino and John Terhune. That gives me the honored distinction to say these are both men of character and have proven by their leadership and multimillion-dollar sales volume in the field that these concepts will work for anyone. They have led thousands and I would proudly recommend these 15 skills to anyone who feels they are missing something in their current training regime. Every chapter will reveal a new discipline of truth and common sense. This book is a winner and so are the authors. You are about to learn something very special. I did and I am a 20-year veteran of the networking industry."
— Scott Kufus, Director of Business Development,
Univera Biosciences

"Never before have two authors extricated and distilled the very essence of building a network marketing business. John and Joe have broken new ground and are charting new territories for today's network marketer. This book is a smart look at what it takes to succeed in this lucrative and exciting business. With practical ideas, insights, and strategies, they have the ability to uncover what appears to be self-evident truths; anyone can make money in an MLM business if they follow a plan. If you are an executive with a network marketing company or considering joining one, this is the only book to read!"
— Sandi Donaldson, President, Moriah Marketing Group

15 SECRETS EVERY NETWORK MARKETER MUST KNOW

Essential Elements and Skills Required to Achieve 6- & 7-Figure Success in Network Marketing

Dr. Joe Rubino
John Terhune

WILEY

John Wiley & Sons, Inc.

Published by John Wiley & Sons, Inc., Hoboken, New Jersey.
Published simultaneously in Canada.

For general information on our other products and services please contact our Customer Care Department within the U.S. at (800) 762-2974, outside the United States at (317) 572-3993 or fax (317) 572-4002.

Wiley also publishes its books in a variety of electronic formats. Some content that appears in print may not be available in electronic books. For more information about Wiley products, visit our web site at www.wiley.com.

Library of Congress Cataloging-in-Publication Data:

Rubino, Joe.
    15 secrets every network marketer must know : essential elements and
  skills required to achieve 6 and 7-figure success in network marketing /
  Joe Rubino, John Terhune.
        p.   cm.
    Published simultaneously in Canada.
    Includes index.
    ISBN-13: 978-0-471-77347-4 (pbk.)
    ISBN-10: 0-471-77347-6
    1. Multilevel marketing—Handbooks, manuals, etc.   I. Title: Fifteen
  secrets every network marketer must know.   II. Terhune, John.   III. Title.
    HF5415.126.R828 2006
    658.8'72—dc22

Printed in the United States of America.

10 9 8 7 6 5 4 3 2 1

Contents

FOREWORD

This book is based upon 33 years of combined experience that Joe Rubino and John Terhune bring to the network marketing profession. Both authors have actual experience in building multimillion dollar network marketing businesses and have achieved success in the top 1 percent in this field. Both came from professional, educated backgrounds. Rubino was a dentist and Terhune a trial attorney. Both excelled in their former professions and brought these success skills to network marketing.

Readers will benefit from the clarity and power of their writing as well as from their actual firsthand experience in knowing what is necessary to reach the highest levels of achievement in the network marketing industry. Every principle offered in the book comes from field-tested and proven experience about what it actually takes to build a successful network. Readers will have confidence in knowing that the instruction given in the pages that follow has proven to create success and continues to prove its value today through actual implementation of the principles discussed. Both authors are widely acknowledged as being among the top network marketing trainers in the world. Both lecture, coach, and train worldwide as well as in North America on a regular basis. This book offers a unique combination of the expertise of these two top trainers and network marketing leaders as they share the secrets to becoming successful in network marketing.

Another element that makes this book unique is that it is the only one on the market that combines the varied approaches of two top trainers with different styles, insights, and methods to support readers' success. Rubino's work combines the disciplines of business productivity with many of the foundational principles of personal development. Terhune's work adds the perspective of an expert in the art of creating motivation and the secrets to a winning attitude. Readers can expect their network marketing businesses to grow as rapidly as they themselves grow personally. They can also expect their self-motivation and attitude to be major contributors to their great success—or lack of it. Woven throughout the book are principles, exercises, and detailed instruction to support readers in their quest to maximize their personal effectiveness, attitude, and behavior as they build their networking dynasties. In this book, Rubino and Terhune put their heads together and speak as one voice so that you, the reader, may prosper from their combined wisdom and insights into what is required to be successful in this great stronghold of free enterprise.

I encourage you to devour the insights Rubino and Terhune offer from their personal business-building experiences. Map each principle onto your business and encourage your team to duplicate each one as well. Doing so will provide you with a duplicable formula for top-shelf success.

Dr. Tom Ventullo
President, www.CenterForPersonalReinvention.com

PREFACE

or more than 50 years, network marketing has offered millions of entrepreneurs the promise of such benefits as the ability to work from home; flexible working hours; the option to engage in the business as much or as little, whenever, and wherever one wants; the ability to escape the corporate rat race, free oneself of bosses and employees, and the potential to generate a continuing royalty-type income that can range from a few hundred dollars monthly to a high six-figure monthly income for an elite, inspirational minority of extraordinary networkers.

Many, often through firsthand experience, see the network marketing concept as the opportunity of a lifetime, the chance for anyone with very little start-up capital (typically $100 to $1,000) to open their own business with the potential to create a life-changing income. Today, the industry of network marketing boasts an impressive, extensive 50+ year track record pointing to numerous companies that have stood the test of time, paying out checks like clockwork monthly to those who have believed in the promise of personal and financial freedom and carried out the mission of network marketing—using the products, recommending them and the income opportunity they make possible, and spreading the word to others interested in generating an income of their own.

Despite this impressive history, many still confuse network marketing with illegal, unethical scams and Ponzi schemes promoted by slick, get-rich-quick charlatans who prey on the naïve and unsuspecting. Although the low start-up costs, lack of educational requirements, and absence of barriers to get going in business make it possible for almost anyone to scrape together a few dollars and start their own network marketing enterprise, this same ease of entry has the majority of people that do become involved not taking the pursuit of their business nearly seriously enough. They do little to learn the critical skills necessary to achieve top-level success; they spend little time becoming educated and trained in these essential success principles; they treat their business as a hobby, often trading in any serious commitment for what is more convenient at the moment; they quit at the first signs of difficulty and rejection; and then they wonder why they had so little success to show for their efforts! And they blame the institution of network marketing for their failures rather than take responsibility for what would be necessary to bring about their own success.

This book was written with a simple, important purpose in mind. It spells out in clear and compelling language the answer to the question "What does it really take for anyone to become successful in the profession of network marketing and to duplicate that success for those they introduce?"

Those of you who have followed the writings of Dr. Joe Rubino know that his other four network marketing books and audio programs each speak to a different aspect of building a successful business with deliberate intention. *The 7-Step System to Building a $1,000,000 Network Marketing Dynasty* spells out in detail a simple, proven system that addresses each area critical to achieving business success: visioning, planning, prospecting, enrolling, training, personal development, and stepping into leadership. Complete with sample visions, letters, faxes, scripts, ads, action plans, personal-development structures, and leadership models, it has been called by network marketing experts the most comprehensive step-by-step manual to take any new distributor from enrollment to leadership duplication.

The Ultimate Guide to Network Marketing is a reflection of Napoleon Hill's mastermind concept. Dozens of top network marketing income earners, trainers, and gurus were asked to share their most preciously guarded principles and concepts they credit for helping them or those they train to achieve the highest levels of accomplishment in our industry. Many of the secrets they share in this book were heretofore only revealed to their own organizations. This book is really 37 mini seminars in one breakthrough-filled volume.

Secrets of Building a Million-Dollar Network Marketing Organization from a Guy Who's Been There Done That and Shows You How You Can Do It Too! has been called the bible of network marketing. It combines proven business-building strategies and insights with personal-effectiveness training, wisdom regarding what it takes to grow personally as rapidly as your business.

Finally, the audio (CD or Cassette) album with workbook, *10 Weeks to Network Marketing Success: The Secrets to Launching Your Very Own Million-Dollar Organization in a 10-Week Business-Building and Personal-Development Self-Study Course*, offers 10 critical lessons that, when mastered, will result in breakthrough achievement. Map a different lesson on each week, and watch your skills and results transform in less than 90 days.

So, why write another book to complement these four? Because it is of vital importance to be able start your new associates off on the right track. *15 Secrets Every Network Marketer Must Know* brings the reader through 15 success distinctions every new person must grasp and every effective leader must teach. These principles can be divided into two basic arenas: state of mind and skills needed to win.

Getting in the right frame of mind begins with the development of a winning attitude. More than any other attribute, a winning attitude will both serve to maximize your charisma quotient, attracting others to you like a magnet, and keep you focused on what's truly important as you go about the building of your network marketing dynasty. Next, the concept of failure is examined. When you learn to embrace and welcome failure, knowing that it is the prerequisite that always accompanies and precedes success in network marketing, it will lose its power to affect you negatively. Failure, after all, is always an interpretation, never a fact. When you can go out and create massive amounts of failure, you'll then learn to create room for the success that inevitably comes to those with a powerful relationship to this concept.

Another foundational principle that all successful networkers possess is self-discipline. In a business where there is no one supervising your every move, it can be all too easy to choose convenience over commitment, comfort over vision. Self-discipline is the internal thermometer that regulates the action machine needed to produce a result. Without it, consistency and persistency give way to sporadic, ineffective behavior more typical of hobbyists than deliberate business builders. Those who possess self-discipline know that quitting is never an option. If it were, perseverance would soon be replaced by resignation. Those who hold quitting as a possible outcome lack a certain expectation in their ultimate success. Because this positive anticipation is lacking, their missing belief in their ultimate victory means that they will eventually sabotage their businesses because they do not expect to make them work. Others will sense this self-doubt and, before long, it will become a self-fulfilling prophecy. When quitting is an option, commitment, creativity, and perseverance are all lacking.

Top network marketers know that productive results are always in line with making the necessary commitments that will cause what they desire to manifest into reality. By choosing daily commitments to those behaviors that will move one's business in a forward direction, rather than taking the path of convenience, success is all but assured. Speaking with a minimum number of prospects daily, weekly, and monthly, becoming adept at inviting people to take a look at the business, showing the plan in a powerful manner, working effectively with upline partners, and duplicating one's productive habits to champion new team members to copy these same behaviors that will bring about winning ways are all a function of following through on a commitment to prospect, enroll, teach, and duplicate effectively.

Of course, all this activity is the byproduct of self-motivation, which results from an expectation of impending success, in other words, a compelling dream or vision that inspires action. Without such a motivating *why* or reason for working the business, it will be all too easy to give into the pressures of life, allowing them to compete with and take precedence over a business focus. Without an inspirational dream to keep one focused and in pursuit, rejection will likely take its toll on morale and the human tendency to seek pleasure (the path of least resistance) and avoid pain (hard work, naysayers, and negative responses).

The ability to maintain the proper frame of mind and elevated spirit conducive to success will most often result from starting the business with the right expectations. Winning distributors know that getting a lot of *no's* is just part of the requirement to get to the *yes's*. They know that building a business is their responsibility; no one is going to do it for them. Developing leaders is a process that takes time and consistent effort. Network marketing is NOT a get-rich-quick scheme. They also realize that it's not for everyone and are thankful for this, knowing that if it were, there would not be an opportunity remaining for them and others before long.

In addition to maintaining such a winning attitude, triumphant networkers realize that their success will be dependent upon them developing the skills necessary to win the networking game. From developing effective prospecting and enrollment skills to training, coaching, challenging, and championing their new associates, this means becoming adept at developing leaders. In fact, they know that this behavior—developing leaders—is what they really are paid to do. The more leaders they are able to duplicate, the bigger their checks will be. They know that leaders are sometimes born and sometimes made, and the best use of their time is to go after those possessing the success skills that have resulted in previous accomplishments in other arenas. By prospecting up (going after thriving individuals and centers of influence), they are more likely to find people who are ready to take on a leadership role.

Flourishing networkers also know that the access to identifying and developing leaders is to become adept at building a perpetual names list. They learn that everyone they know or know of will go on that list but they will use list finesse to first target the candidates most likely to achieve success. They understand that maintaining the right posture is so important to attracting the right people; it's like playing chess—you make a move then your prospect or new associate makes a move. Top networkers know that it pays to only work with the willing, never displaying any signs of desperation or attachment to any particular prospect needing to join their business. You can't push a rope and you can't get unmotivated and uninspired people to do what it takes to win, even if you want success for them more than they want it for themselves.

Furthermore, associates with a winning attitude realize that network marketing is a contact sport, not for the weak or faint of heart. Those who will succeed know that this success will come about from massive, effective, consistent, and persistent action, coupled with a willingness to immerse themselves into personal development, always looking for what worked and what was missing that, if put into place, would maximize their personal effectiveness and productivity.

They know that effective action means making professional presentations that tell prospects that they are being offered a rare and special opportunity to partner with business professionals that are on the certain track to personal and financial freedom, and if they join them, they, too, can be on that same track. Top network marketers take on the challenge of becoming adept at showing the plan. They also understand that this requires time and practice. Rather than seeking perfection, they choose excellence, knowing that, with practice and feedback, each subsequent presentation will be better than their last. And, of course, the best presentation is usually a waste of time without timely, persistent follow-up. Strange as it may seem, even open-minded, interested prospects will usually not call to express their interest—they must be followed up with in a prompt and professional manner. As all leading money earners know, the fortune is truly in the follow-up!

Lastly, all successful people in any field, and especially top network marketers, know that there is no arriving. The path to success is an infinite trail, a process without end. It involves a willingness to stay in a continual state of personal development. It requires a desire to remain in an everlasting state of inquiry, more concerned with the perpetual questions that will certainly arise for those courageous enough to ask them. This inquisitive, open attitude will lead to growth and insights into areas where one was previously blind, rather than looking for some definitive answer that limits further inquiry and expansion. True leaders know that there will always be more information to learn and greater wisdom to glean; further enriching achievements to explore; and new and upcoming leaders to inspire, champion, contribute to, and impact.

As you take on these 15 concepts that will surely cause your network marketing dynasty to grow and prosper, I invite you to remember the three elements essential for any meaningful accomplishment: You must produce a result, you must experience personal growth, and just as importantly, you must have fun along the way. May you share the precious gift of network marketing with many who go on to duplicate your success, thus ensuring a better world for us all.

Yours in partnership and success,

Joe Rubino
John Terhune

ACKNOWLEDGMENTS

This book is dedicated to my wife, Janice, for her encouragement, support, and perpetual love, and to my longtime friend and business partner, Dr. Tom Ventullo. Tom and I entered this great opportunity of network marketing in 1991, retiring from our dental practice together, both at age 37. Tom taught me the meaning of partnership, being the first of thousands of other partners who followed in our business. Our partnership continues to this day as co-founders of The Center for Personal Reinvention, an organization committed to the excellence and success of others.

—Joe Rubino
CEO, www.CenterForPersonalReinvention.com

My dedication as always honors my God, who has blessed me with a phenomenal wife—who is my best friend, great children, family, and friends, and a continuously burning fire within to be better tomorrow than I was today.

—John Terhune

ABOUT THE AUTHORS

Dr. Joe Rubino is an internationally acclaimed network marketing trainer, author, success coach, and the CEO of The Center for Personal Reinvention, an organization that provides personal and group coaching as well as productivity and leadership development courses. Dr. Joe retired from his successful million-dollar dental practice at the age of 37, having replaced and exceeded his professional income with a network marketing residual income. He was featured on the cover of several leading publications including *Success Magazine* and in the cover story, *We Create Millionaires: How Network Marketing's Entrepreneurial Elite Are Building Fortunes at Breakneck Speed* because of his ability to champion others to succeed. Joe is the author of 10 international best sellers, currently in 19 languages and 49 countries. They include:

- *The 7-Step System to Building a $1,000,000 Network Marketing Dynasty: How to Achieve Financial Independence through Network Marketing*
- *The Ultimate Guide to Network Marketing: 37 Top Network Marketing Income-Earners Share Their Most Preciously Guarded Secrets to Building Extreme Wealth*
- *Secrets of Building a Million-Dollar Network Marketing Organization from a Guy Who's Been There Done That, and Shows You How You Can Do It Too!*
- *The Magic Lantern: A Fable about Leadership, Personal Excellence, and Empowerment*
- *Restore Your Magnificence: A Life-Change Guide to Reclaiming Your Self-Esteem*

- *The Legend of the Light-Bearers: A Fable About Personal Reinvention and Global Transformation*
- *10 Weeks to Network Marketing Success: The Secrets to Launching Your Very Own Million-Dollar Organization in a 10-Week Business-Building and Personal-Development Self-Study Course*
- *Secret #1: Self-Motivation Affirmation Tapes*

Joe is now committed to supporting others to enjoy successful lives and businesses. His vision is to impact the lives of 20 million people to be prosperous and live without regrets. For information about The Center for Personal Reinvention and its services or to order any of Dr. Joe's books or tapes, visit http://www.CenterForPersonalReinvention.com. To contact Dr. Joe about the possibility of hiring him as your personal success coach, e-mail: DrJRubino@email.com or call 888-821-3135.

John Terhune is the founder and CEO of Rainmaker Consulting Services. Before reaching levels that put him in the top 1/100th of 1 percent of all of the people who have ever come into the network marketing industry, John spent the better part of a decade as a prosecuting attorney in the State of Florida. In law school he was named the best trial advocate in the United States in a trial competition sponsored by the American Trial Lawyers Association. As the chief felony prosecutor of his judicial circuit, he won 232 of 241 cases tried in front of a jury. While executing his duties as a prosecuting attorney, he simultaneously acted as an adjunct instructor at multiple law schools, universities, and law-enforcement academies.

John saw the network marketing opportunity in the late 1980s and promptly went to work. Within 24 months he was well into a six-figure income in his network marketing opportunity, and within three and a half years was qualifying at the top level in his company's pay plan, where he maintained an ultrasuccessful organization for seven consecutive years before starting his consulting, writing, and coaching careers.

His consulting career started as the result of a phone call during which a publicly traded network marketing company asked him to consult with them and help their management team work in greater harmony with their field leaders. This started as a series of clients seeking consulting services and eventually led to John starting his consulting firm Rainmaker Consulting Services. Rainmaker Consulting Services employs 10 people and works closely with clients that range from start-ups to well established companies who are looking to take their results to the next level. Rainmaker has developed state-of-the-art applications for the network marketing industry and owns several technology applications, including a digital learning system, that are exclusive to Rainmaker in the network marketing setting. His clients are located throughout the globe, including Russia, Europe, Singapore, and North America. John's expertise extends to the areas of business-model development, compensation-plan design, strategic planning and execution, funding, the creation of marketing-support materials and growth strategies that include creating the infrastructure of training systems that will support short- and long-term growth.

John has taken time out of his busy schedule to author several books and training programs that are industry guideposts for success in business and network marketing. His audio program *Basic Training* is used by thousands of network marketers each year as a foundation to growing a significant downline organization.

John's brainchild, Attitude Pump www.attitudepump.com has become one of the fastest growing communities in the world. Through this property, he has taken the lead as the most articulate spokesman for the power of a great attitude. His newest book *Decide to Have a Great Day* is a highly acclaimed compendium of life lessons regarding the power of a great attitude.

John's book *The True Entrepreneur* www.thetrue entrepreneur.com has been described by Dr. Denis Waitley as, "the definitive work on the subject of entrepreneurship."

John serves on the board of directors for multiple network marketing companies and has acted as legal counsel and strategic advisor for multiple start-up and well-established companies.

PART ONE

GETTING IN THE RIGHT FRAME OF MIND

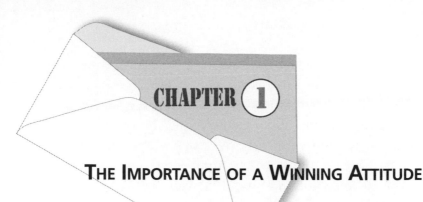

THE IMPORTANCE OF A WINNING ATTITUDE

There are two traits that separate high achievers from those people who go through life settling for what life gives them. These two qualities distinguish the people who make life happen from those who passively allow life to happen to them. The two traits that make a huge difference in your ability to achieve the desires of your heart are a positive attitude and self-discipline.

Let's begin by talking about attitude, clearly one of the most powerful resources available to any human being. A person's attitude transcends, in either a positive or a negative way, every part of his or her life. It affects their relationships, physical and mental energy, stamina, self-image, work habits, willingness to take risks, willingness to try something new and challenging, their ability to deal with stressful situations, degree of happiness and, of course, their ability to achieve beyond their current circumstances.

A person with average talents and a great attitude will triumph over the enormously talented person with a bad or

3

even an average attitude. Of all of the physical and mental traits possessed by human beings that separate one person from the next, attitude stands alone as the great divider between average performance and peak achievement.

Men and women who truly work at creating, and then protecting, a great attitude will ultimately achieve far more than people who do not understand the vital nature of this ingredient for success. But what exactly is a positive attitude? And how does one acquire it?

A positive attitude is a disciplined decision to maintain a consistently confident expectation of good results.

In essence, it is faith in the realization of a bright present and an even brighter future. A positive attitude is not, as some think, psyching yourself up to believe that the fairy godmother will come to your rescue, or that some miraculous breakthrough, like winning the lottery, will reverse your current fortunes. The proper mental outlook is based on faith — faith that life is inherently phenomenal and that you will, if you persevere with a positive expectation of your ultimate success, realize your dream in the end.

You should regard your attitude as an enormously valuable asset that deserves and demands careful protection. When you leave your house, you probably lock your doors to protect your possessions from thieves. However, did you ever stop to think that you could lose all those tangible assets and reacquire them ten times over if you were to develop and maintain the right attitude?

Just about everyone can sustain a positive mind-set when things are going well, and we are all prone to discouragement when things are not progressing smoothly. One of the secrets to being happy is learning how to keep your attitude from being on a roller coaster. Anyone can be up when things are going in their favor and anyone can be down when adversity strikes. However, the person who will be the happiest is the one who can be up when others, possessing a lesser attitude, would be down as a result of the challenges that life happens to offer.

Discipline yourself to understand that you have the sole responsibility for your mental outlook. There are innumerable issues that present themselves every day that conspire to pollute your positive attitude: discordant family relationships, money troubles, unhappy employees, rude customers, the business environment . . . even something as trivial as the traffic you encounter on the drive to work. If you allow the circumstances of life to determine your attitude, think of what you'll become! The only thing that separates victory from defeat at these critical moments is a disciplined, positive attitude that has been purposefully developed over the years.

A positive attitude, then, is a personal decision to believe the best about yourself and your dreams. It is a mental step of faith whereby you confidently assume that the day's events will validate your expectation of good results. Maintaining a positive attitude isn't always easy! It demands continual vigilance; you can't fly on autopilot. You will have to work on it every day, but there are few things in life that will pay you greater dividends.

HOW TO DEVELOP A GREAT ATTITUDE

One of the greatest things anyone can say about you is that you have a *phenomenal attitude*. You will get the attention of other human beings in whatever arena you are working, and you will separate yourself from the crowd if you exude a great attitude. A superior attitude gets noticed in a positive way, just as a poor attitude gets noticed in a negative way. Whether you are at work, home, or play, you will shine brighter and create far more opportunities for yourself in life if you exhibit a winning attitude. Now that we have defined what a great attitude is, let's cover what you have to do to develop one.

The best way to raise the attitude of people around you is to exude an exceptional attitude yourself. People should feel better about themselves and life after spending time with you. This effect is impossible to achieve without an exemplary attitude that says, "I am happy about who I am, where I am going, and my expectations of the future."

There are several steps to creating an attitude that will be the foundation for a continuous path to achievement.

Work Hard at Feeling Good about Yourself

How you feel about yourself has a tremendous impact on your attitude. Your view of yourself creates the basis for your attitude. If you feel lazy, unproductive, or out of shape, you won't respect yourself because of your lack of discipline, you won't have confidence in yourself because of the way you handle difficult times that you encounter, and you won't have a sense of inner worth or believe deeply in your integrity.

Conversely, if you feel good about the way you look and perform, if you have an inner confidence resulting from the fact that you exercise self-discipline, if you have confidence in the way that you handle difficult situations, if you know that within you is a reservoir of determination that will get you through any challenge, and you know that you are a person of integrity, then a great attitude is a natural extension of this view of yourself.

Each day presents a new opportunity to create positive experiences that merit a deepened sense of self-confidence. You have total control of what your self-image and self-confidence will be. It takes time, but you can establish an entirely new foundation of trusting your instincts for success, making the right decisions, taking chances, preparing, practicing, persevering, and winning. You can do whatever it takes for you to develop that unconscious swagger that comes from feeling good about the person you are and possessing a solid belief in your own potential.

The ability to exhibit a great attitude has a lot to do with your self-image. For an in-depth self-study course on how to complete your troubled past, assess your present state, and design a compelling future based on high self-esteem, see *Restore Your Magnificence: A Life-Changing Guide to Reclaiming Your Self-Esteem* by Joe Rubino.

What actions can you take to make sure that this building block to a great attitude is in place? Here are some suggestions.

Get on a Regular Program of Exercise and Eat a Proper Diet

The better the physical shape you are in, the easier it is for you to feel good about yourself. Feeling good about yourself physically puts a special bounce in your step and leads to a confident expectation regarding what you will attract in your life. A great attitude is much more likely to grow in the fertile soil of feeling good about your health and physical appearance. A regular exercise and eating regimen takes discipline. Any time that you exercise self-discipline, you overcome the voice inside of you that urges you to take the path of least resistance and the least pain. The more you wage that battle and the more that you win that battle, the better you will feel about yourself.

Associate with People Who Will Be Fertile Ground for a Great Attitude

It is a fact that most of us adopt and reflect the attitudes of those with whom we associate regularly. "Bad company corrupts good morals," the proverb reads. In the very same way, associating with people who are consistently negative will corrupt a previously good attitude. We know the effect that a bad relationship can have on children's behavior. As parents, we guard that aspect of their lives zealously because we know the influence of a positive relationship as opposed to a negative association.

Be just as zealous in choosing your own relationships, because they will have a dramatic effect on your personal attitude. Surely, there have been times when you have been around someone who acted like a drain on your battery because they were always complaining and seeing the negative in everything. Conversely, recall when you have been in the presence of someone so positive that their view of the world and circumstances of their life just inspired you.

The truth is you can't afford to be around people who drain your energy if you expect to create and maintain a great attitude. You need to associate with people who energize you and charge your battery, not drain it. Every day, you have a choice about the people you associate with. Each good decision you make here will add another valuable brick in the foundation you lay in building a stellar attitude.

Write down the names of the five most positive people you know. These people don't rob you of your energy or leave you feeling the same or worse when they leave; they leave you feeling charged and optimistic, expecting great things.

Now write down the names of the five most negative people that you know. These people don't leave you feeling the same either. They leave you feeling drained; their very nature leaves you with less air in your balloon than when you first got together.

Now, write down next to each of their names how much time you typically spend with each of them. Here is what this exercise is all about. You need to become very aware of who the people are with whom you are spending most of your time, and determine if they truly serve you and boost your attitude or detract from it.

From this point forward, maximize the time you spend with those people who invigorate you, and minimize the time you spend with those who drain your battery. You will be pleasantly surprised by the positive effect this will have on your ability to create and maintain a great attitude. The moment you surrender ownership of your attitude to circumstances or to another person, you compromise its power in your life and risk its loss.

Read the types of books and listen to those audio programs that fill your mind with enlightened information that lends itself to the creation and maintenance of a great attitude. Develop an insatiable appetite for positive mental nutrition. Begin to view your travel time as attitude maintenance time. Think about the hours that you spend in your car or commuting every year. What if you made a mental decision to make this time personal-development and attitude-maintenance time? How many hours did you waste last year listening to some silly radio station, or reading material that had no impact on the incredibly valuable asset called your attitude?

Our minds need positive input every day. If we feast on a diet of positive mental food on a regular basis, our minds react favorably and support our cause with a high degree of energy and resilience. The best thing about this diet is that you don't have to count calories! The more positive mental input you take in every day, the better.

If you want to have the type of attitude that is the foundation for achievement, make the mental decision that your state of mind is just as, or more important than, your physical well-being. Take care of it; invest in it. Read about inspirational people and the attitudes that they exhibited on their way to their great accomplishments. Get into the heads of people who have accomplished what you want to accomplish by listening to CDs, reading books, subscribing to newsletters, going to seminars . . . whatever it takes to put you in a mode of continuous growth. Make a decision that the person you are going to be next month will be more evolved and possess a better attitude than the person you are this month.

Dare to Dream about a Better Tomorrow

People who are on a mission to accomplish great things find having a great attitude much easier because such an attitude comes with a high degree of expectation for a better tomorrow. If you know that tomorrow is going to be no better than today, it is hard to be optimistic in mood and activity. A great many people are trying to achieve goals, but face a problem that can be clearly defined: They have not tied the desires of their hearts to the activity they are about to undertake! They just don't have the right mental attitude to be effective.

Maintain a positive perspective by reconnecting to your dreams on a daily basis. Allow your vision for success to act in the same way as a ground wire does for a lightning rod. Think of your mind as the lightning rod. The negative things that inevitably occur in life and business strike at your thoughts, just as the lightning strikes the lightning rod. However, no matter how powerful the bolt, its force is neutralized because the ground wire carries the electricity (negativity) harmlessly away.

Throughout your life, bolts of lightning will strike at you. You will experience setbacks and temporary failures. Faced with crushing disappointment, the average person is rocked back on his or her heels. Many never recover. They quietly sink into the quicksand of despair and ultimately accept defeat. However, if you have a dream of which you are in passionate pursuit, you will have a far deeper ability to be resilient in your response to situations that would otherwise affect your attitude in a negative way.

Have a Personal Mission and Values Statement That Will Allow You to Reconnect with Your Vision for Your Life

Create written values, mission, and vision statements, which spell out who you are and what you want your life to become, and keep them close at hand for regular review. (See *The 7-Step System to Building a $1,000,000 Network Marketing Dynasty* for a clear explanation on creating a compelling, values-based vision for your life and business.) When a setback has left you momentarily disheartened, pull out your written statements and remind yourself of the person you are and of the emotionally compelling vision you are working to achieve. This will help you to refocus on your ultimate destination and reconnect with your passion.

Have an Attitude of Gratitude

Another ingredient to add to the recipe for maintaining a persistently positive attitude is a perspective of gratitude. In our society, we are constantly bombarded with messages about what we don't have. Despite all these negative messages, the simple truth is that every man, woman, and child wakes up to potential abundance every day. Every person could be bubbling over with excitement about today and tomorrow, but most are not. Being grateful for what you *do* have will help you radiate positive energy. After all, who do you tend to notice first in a social gathering? Who do people gravitate toward and engage in conversation? It is invariably the person with the positive outlook and enthusiastic attitude. Work hard to make that person be you!

Live Life with Passion

There is no more rewarding way to experience life than by living in the passionate pursuit of your dreams. Choose to work passionately to bring about your ideal vision for a dream life, because that is when you are the most alive and when you exhibit a great attitude.

Wake up every morning with an exciting expectation for a greater tomorrow. If you have lost or have never had that feeling, it may be time to move on and re-envision a new and more inspiring future for yourself and for those you love. Examine your life, your associations, and your actions. Move toward crafting a compelling dream. When you have crafted a dream that motivates and inspires you and you are engaged in the passionate pursuit of that dream, you glow as if you are on fire. Now is the time to decide to come alive!

For further information and inspiration specific to the development, maintenance, and protection of a great attitude see *Decide to Have a Great Day* by John Terhune.

CHAPTER 2

THE POWER OF FAILURE

One of the most valuable experiences that you can have in your life is failure. How you handle failure is another area where you can dramatically separate yourself from the crowd.

Building a home-based business is more about failure than it is about winning day after day. Without a willingness to experience failure, you will not create the room to do what it takes to also experience success. Home-based businesses are also about sales. In reality, most everything in business is ultimately about sales. Whether you are selling your product, your concept, or yourself, you are in a constant state of sales in the network marketing industry. Because you are in the sales business, you are going to get turned down (fail) far more times than you are going to win. It's just part of the winning process.

There is a classic scene in the timeless movie, *It's a Wonderful Life* with Jimmy Stewart. Two angels are discussing the urgent mission to visit Earth and help George Bailey. "What's wrong?" the first angel asks. "Is he sick?" The second angel replies, "No, it's worse than that; he's discouraged." George saw his life as a failure, largely due to a combination of circumstances that conspired to keep him from realizing his boyhood dream of traveling the world. Although he interpreted the path his life took instead of traveling the globe as one of failure, he got to see that many others viewed his life as a resounding success, much to the contrary. Failure is always an interpretation rather than a factual experience.

Setbacks *will* happen, and they can be painful. Therefore, rather than viewing failure as a deadly enemy that destroys your dreams, learn to change your perspective. Teach yourself to see failure as an important *ally*, which increases your knowledge and builds your internal fortitude. Indeed, failure has tremendous value. As General Colin Powell has said, "Perpetual opposition is a force multiplier."

People who achieve great things are not afraid to fail. This is because they recognize that failure is an excellent teacher when it is viewed through the eyes of a winner. As children, we fell down countless times while learning to walk; today we walk around all day without even giving the task conscious thought. Thomas Edison failed more than a thousand times before he invented a working light bulb; today he is remembered as a great inventor, not a great failure. Babe Ruth struck out more than a thousand times, yet he is called The Sultan of Swat to this day, not The Wizard of Whiff.

Neither Edison nor Ruth was some kind of human anomaly, possessing some vastly superior mental or physical ability that separated them from all other mortals. Thomas Edison is well-known for dryly observing that "Genius is one percent inspiration, and ninety-nine percent perspiration." What *does* set winners apart from the average individual is that *they treat failure as an event, not a destiny*. All successful achievers know that a crucial key to moving on toward victory is being willing to face down failure along the way. If we learn to see failure as a signpost that points us toward success, we understand that giving ourselves freedom to fail creates the opportunities for big wins.

Everyone has experienced failures and lived to tell about them. We learn from our failures and use them to add to our base of knowledge. As a tiny baby, the very first time you reached for an object and inadvertently pushed it away from you, your mind was busily processing information that would allow you to successfully grasp that object on a later attempt. Your failure actually made you more effective.

When you experience failure, there are several things you can do to turn your discouragement into determination. First, make time to study the attitudes and actions of those who have earned great victories in your world. Read the biographies of men and women who have overcome adversity and gone on to great success. The more you see how other people experienced similar struggles in their early years, the more you will reinforce your determination to push past whatever discouragement or setback you are experiencing.

A second way to turn discouragement into determination is to find a coach or a mentor who will help you keep your attitude where it needs to be. A good coach or mentor will help you keep both failures and successes in perspective. For additional information on personal or group coaching programs tailored to champion the success of network marketers, visit www.CenterForPersonalReinvention.com or www.rainmaker consulting.com.

Third, you will turn discouragement into determination when you create written values, mission, and vision statements, which spell out who you are and what you want your life to become, and keep them close at hand for regular review. When a setback has left you momentarily disheartened, pull out your written statements and remind yourself of who you are and of the emotionally compelling vision you are working to achieve. This will help you refocus on your ultimate destination and re-connect with your passion. A powerful values-based vision can fuel the necessary self-motivation required to burn through any temporary setbacks. Again, for a detailed guide to creating a vision that can motivate you and inspire others, see Step 1 of *The 7-Step System to Building a $1,000,000 Network Marketing Dynasty* by Dr. Joe Rubino.

Fourth, you will turn discouragement into determination by developing a method that enables you to put things in perspective at will. Whether you take a drive, listen to soothing music, go for a walk, or engage in strenuous exercise, you should create a mechanism that offers a way to return your thoughts to a place where mental clarity and confidence in your vision are restored and reinforced.

Finally, and most importantly, you will turn discouragement into great triumphs by developing the right attitude toward failure. A failure should trigger a careful, moment-by-moment examination of the thinking, planning, and actions that led up to the failure. Painstakingly seek to identify what has gone wrong, so that when you face similar circumstances in the future, you will be more effective. You will always learn more from failure than from victory. Get into the habit of dissecting each failure to analyze what may have been missing that, if put into place next time, would possibly lead to a much different outcome.

If you allow your mistakes to stop you from moving forward, you've allowed failure to have the victory. Why in the world would you give the potential for failure, or failure itself, that much power over your destiny? Don't do it! Harness the power of failure and continue to pursue your dream.

Consider the following analogy. For you to make your dreams happen as a result of your business opportunity, you are going to have to fill up two containers with water. One container is a 55-gallon drum. This drum has a big sign on the front that says No! The other container is a one-gallon container that has a sign on it that says Yes! Both containers must be filled for you to be successful. Every time you show your opportunity or make a contact, you get a glass of water to put into your containers. Being rejected is a good thing because you have to fill up the No container. Making a sale or sponsoring someone gives you a glass of water for your Yes container. You need many more no's than yes's to be successful.

SUCCESS IN ANY TYPE OF SALES IS A NUMBERS GAME

There are a certain number of contacts, a certain number of business presentations, a certain number of follow-up meetings that you will need to make the numbers produce your win, but it is still largely a numbers game. How large the numbers will have to be will depend on your ability to relate to people and your ability to convey confidence in your opportunity. The more effective you become in creating value for your prospects, the fewer people you will need to speak with to produce the same result. Keeping your focus on your expectations, it is important to remember that nothing you could ever offer will always be exciting to everyone. When you took on your business opportunity, you saw the vision for what was possible to achieve. You got it. It was crystal clear to you. Because you realized it, you naturally thought that everyone else was going to get it as easily as you did.

Well, back to reality . . . everyone else is not going to get it right away. Many will never get it. Realize that, when you saw your opportunity, you were looking at the opportunity at a particular time in your life through the glasses of your experiences in life up to that time. No one's experiences are just like yours. How you are feeling about life and how frustrated you are about where you are in relation to the effort that you put in those circumstances are unique to you.

Whether you realized it or not, you were in the *looking zone* because the circumstances of your life were such that you were beginning to think about taking a different path. The attributes of a home-based business opportunity (small capital outlay, investment of your spare time, the potential of substantial residual income) were all issues that were compelling to you because of where you were in your life.

If someone says no to your opportunity, they are not saying no to you. They are saying no to the opportunity right now. If you treat the person with respect and leave them with a positive experience from your contact with them, there may be a time when they will be ready. Never take rejection personally, they are not rejecting you, they are only rejecting the opportunity right now!

Keep something else in mind as you put your expectations in place. There are some people in our world that are just negative. It doesn't matter what you show them, they are not going to do something about their lives. There are some people who would rather be miserable because it gives them an excuse to complain. If they were happy, they wouldn't have anything to complain about and that would make them miserable, too. They are out there, and you will run into them. Don't allow them to ruin your day and don't take their cynicism personally. Their rejection is about them, not you. All you can do is offer the great gift that your income opportunity can be to those who see it for what it is and act upon it. If your prospect decides not to accept your gift, it does not diminish the value of the gift in any way. Just remember to treat everyone with respect, and preserve the opportunity for a later relationship.

You are now in the right frame of mind to really build your business. Let's recap what this frame of mind looks like. You know that the only thing standing between you and your dream is filling two containers with water. Each action that you take toward building your business represents a glass of water that you will pour into one of two containers, and both containers must be filled. The No container is 55 gallons in size and the Yes container is only one gallon big, *but* you must fill *both*. You are going to be as excited about a no as you will a yes because you need a lot more no's than yes's! You realize that not everyone is in the looking zone, and that no one business plan is for everyone.

Putting yourself in the right frame of mind will minimize fear or apprehension. A little fear or apprehension is a good thing. It gets some important juices flowing in your heart and your head. If you were to talk to any professional who has to perform a task, the vast majority of them will tell you they still have initial jitters or butterflies before they take center stage. Whether it is a professional golfer on the first tee, or a newscaster getting ready to begin broadcast of the 6 P.M. news, they still get butterflies. Professionals teach the butterflies to fly in formation.

Fear can be almost eliminated with sufficient practice and preparation. Usually, fear comes from the fact that you think someone will laugh at you or not respect what you are doing. You must think properly about your opportunity. No one can laugh at the potential for success in the network marketing world. The network marketing industry has produced thousands of millionaires over the past thirty years.

Anyone who really understands the business world has to respect the fact that, for a minuscule amount of money, you have the potential for a huge financial home run. We tend to make reference to only those people who have hit the ball completely out of the park. The truth is there are tens, possibly even hundreds, of thousands of people in our industry who make fantastic incomes without having to fight a traffic jam on the way to work. They work part time at home, take time off when they want, and don't worry about needing to answer to a boss. If anyone really knew the truth about our industry, they would find it impossible to be anything short of very impressed.

You need to give yourself a bit of credit for what you have done. You have evaluated your situation in life and have said, "I can do better." The fact that you took action on your situation, and decided to do something about it separates you considerably from the crowd.

Be proud of your decision to become an entrepreneur, and be proud that you have the foresight and courage to take your destiny into your own hands. Anyone can show up and report to a boss every day. Anyone can allow someone else to determine the value of his or her efforts. It takes serious guts to risk failure and to make it based on the merits of your own efforts. By your decision to begin your own business, you have answered a call to be an entrepreneur. You are acting on your dreams. You should be very proud of yourself and what you are doing.

Practice in all areas of your business will serve to take away fear or apprehension. This is where it is important to realize that regardless of whether you are failing, don't worry. Every time you do anything connected with building your business, you are practicing your skills. Those who see the big picture understand that failures are merely temporary setbacks on the road to ultimate success. The only people who fail in network marketing are those who quit before identifying their first leader!

If you are brand new, set a goal to show 100 prospects your opportunity, with no attachment to sponsoring anyone into your business. Be willing to be a novice and enjoy the learning process until you get good at mastering your new chosen profession!

CHAPTER ③

SELF-DISCIPLINE—THE SINGLE MOST IMPORTANT PREREQUISITE FOR SUCCESS

Self-discipline just doesn't sound like fun, does it? Most people equate anything to do with discipline with pain and suffering, like fingernails dragging across a chalkboard. Hearing the word *discipline* almost makes you want to rebel, as though you were a school kid who knows that it must mean trouble.

Recognize that self-discipline has the potential of being one of your greatest assets. It offers the ability to distinguish you from your competition. It can make all of the difference for you in every area of your life.

Your willingness to apply self-discipline to your life will separate you from the average person, as clearly as the difference between a great attitude and a terrible one. This is one of those areas in life where you have the ability to choose which side of the line you want to live on. You can live on the side that exercises self-discipline or the side that exercises immediate gratification with no thought about the long-term consequences of your actions or inactions. Which side of the

23

line you choose on a moment-by-moment basis will have a direct effect on the quality of your life and the magnitude of your achievements. This is an area of your life just like attitude, where you can have total control if you make the decision to exercise it.

Self-discipline is about making a decision or choice to deny yourself pleasure at the moment in trade for a better moment sometime in the future. Inherent in the concept of self-discipline is a willingness to opt for delayed gratification versus instant satisfaction. Or, said another way, it is a willingness to listen to the voice that opts for excellence instead of settling for just being average

Exercise is an area where many people struggle with self-discipline. Choosing *not* to exercise is certainly more convenient and will feel better for the moment. However, that moment will soon pass, and you will have to face yourself and admit that you took the easy way that created fleeting pleasure, instead of the results you really desire in the long run. When you exercise consistently, you sacrifice today in order to bring about a future achievement. It is *not* about how you feel today that is important; it is the long-term benefits of exercising versus the short-term gratification realized by not working out.

You will have a higher degree of satisfaction in your life and will accomplish so much more as a human being if you learn how to discipline your decisions with a long-term perspective. In other words, as you make decisions, you must consider the long-term consequences of the decision that you are making that moment. Every decision you make today, to act or not, will have future ramifications.

Your ability to exercise self-discipline is dramatically increased if you have goals in your life that motivate you to be in action with an expectation that these actions will be productive in bringing about your desired results. If you have a goal to be in shape, if you have a goal to be respected by your peers, if you have a goal of personal excellence in business or in your personal life, the goal puts the immediate decision in a different framework. Having a goal gives special purpose to each decision. If the decision specific to that action has no anchor such as a goal or a dream, there is no purpose in the moment other than that enemy of success called instant gratification.

Consider the following example. Sitting in front of you is your favorite type of pie. You have had plenty to eat but that pie certainly does look good. You might be persuaded to rationalize that it is not that big of a deal because it is not a big piece. However, you resist, because you know that you stay thin one meal at a time, and you get fat one meal at a time. Self-discipline in the areas of eating and exercise tends to transcend all areas of life. You need to implement the same mental willpower about diet or exercise as you would about whether to pick up the phone and call your prospect or watch *Survivor* on television.

You don't get in shape with the next workout alone. You get in shape as the result of honoring a discipline of daily workouts over time. The skipping of workouts over time keeps you out of shape. The skipping of this workout produces immediate gratification. To get into shape or to build a successful business, you must learn to exercise delayed gratification and self-discipline, choosing the actions that support your goals over immediate gratification. Self-discipline is a mental choice to opt for the long-term results of each day's many important decisions instead of the short-term results that come from taking the easy way out.

Why is the exercise of self-discipline so tough? It is really very simple. There are two voices in your head that have *easy* and *pleasure* as defaults. Every human being has the same default as part of his or her genetic makeup. What makes self-discipline tough is that you must create a voice inside of you that decides to override the pleasure in the moment, spurning the genetic default for instant gratification. Now the good news about this dynamic is that it is your choice with every decision, every single day of your life. Do you listen to the voice within that cries out for pleasure in the moment, or do you create a voice called character that has the ability to override the voice that calls for immediate gratification?

Character and self-discipline have a significant connection within the complicated makeup of each human being. Do people who lack self-discipline also lack character? No. However, character is often the foundation for self-discipline. Over time, the exercise of self-discipline and delayed gratification will create self-confidence and a positive self-image. You will come to know that you can depend upon yourself to make the right decisions, the decisions that honor your vision for your life over what is most convenient for you to do, but not in your best interests at the moment.

It is important to realize that if you are in business today, appearance counts. Keep in mind, however, that appearance has to do with more than the clothes you are wearing and the makeup you have on. Your daily habits that reflect self-discipline (or not) will speak volumes to other people about who you are. People are much quicker to respect, believe in, and follow someone who exercises self-discipline and delayed gratification than someone who lives just for the moment with no strong sense of commitment to greater goals and dreams.

Your ability to call on the voice within to help you exercise the necessary self-discipline to bring about a desired result has a lot to do with whether you are sufficiently motivated by a vision large enough to move you in the direction of your dreams. If you have something that you want very much, the decision to opt for delayed gratification is much easier than if the decision has no link to something that is emotionally important to your heart.

A simple mental phenomenon happens when people exercise great self-discipline. They feel the automatic, genetic call for pleasure in the moment, like everyone else. However, because they have strengthened their ability to pause and reflect upon the outcomes that their decisions will produce, they have claimed the personal power necessary to act in a manner consistent with their mission in that particular area of their lives. They have also created the mental ability to out-rationalize the voice that opts for pleasure in the moment. You see, that voice that opts for pleasure in the moment is terribly persuasive. He or she has the ability to craft a compelling argument supported with facts and examples to justify taking the lower road. This voice is a master of compromise that supports the road that leads to pleasure in the moment, while selling out the probability of realizing the more important larger vision for what is possible.

There are four applications of self-discipline that can pay huge dividends:

1. *Be punctual*. People have destroyed their credibility with business associates by not applying self-discipline with respect to being on time for appointments. When you have scheduled an appointment with someone, whether on the phone or in person, being on time tells the other person that you respect the value of their time because you were willing to prioritize your engagement with them. Being late for an appointment sends a deafening message that you do not respect their time and that your time has

more value than theirs. It is better to be very early, rather than being even slightly late. By exercising self-discipline in this area of your life, you will be sending the message that you honor your word and your commitments. Witnessing this behavior in you will more likely motivate others to follow your example and respect the time of others as well.

2. *Do not procrastinate.* Procrastination is the by-product of a lack of discipline. Each day, compile a list of things that must be done by the end of the day. Then, prioritize the things you want to do the least, with an intention to get to them first. Attack the things that you want to do least with as much enthusiasm as you can, reminding yourself of the reasons they are important to accomplish. The rest of the items on your list will seem easier when the things you dread are done.

3. *Maintain good physical health and appearance.* Discipline in this area actually transcends and makes the application of self-discipline in all other areas of your life much easier. If you exercise self-discipline in the areas of eating and exercise, you will be developing the willpower that can be successfully applied to other areas of life. The application of self-discipline is very much like the strengthening of a muscle. The more you use and apply it, the more you experience its benefits and the easier it is to opt for delayed gratification.

4. *Maintain a strong work ethic.* This is an area that can separate you from the crowd in the network marketing world. Many people are willing to work hard for a short while but few people are willing to work hard for an extended time. By demonstrating a strong work ethic, you will inspire others to follow your example. A concentrated effort

resulting in massive action and subsequent accelerated business growth will generate a residual income that will allow for plenty of time to enjoy the finer things in life once your organization develops leaders. The activity of duplicating your efforts by developing other committed, self-motivated leaders will cause your organization to take on a life of its own that no longer eventually requires your hard work.

Self-discipline results in many benefits, both tangible and intangible:

- Self-respect
- Self-confidence
- An attractive energy of confidence about you that reflects self-respect, self-confidence, and belief in your eventual success that will draw people to you like a magnet
- Momentum in your life and business
- Because the exercise of self-discipline is a habit, this same habit will transcend all other areas of your life

Today you will face dozens of moments where you will be able to experience short-term pleasure in the moment or opt for the better decision that will set the foundation for a long-term benefit. If you expect to join the ranks of elite performers in network marketing, you are going to have to do what the peak performers do to get into that zone. The top income earners in our profession choose self-discipline and delayed gratification over convenience and immediate satisfaction.

Take a moment and consider how you stand in terms of being self-disciplined. Go through the areas that were listed and on a 1-to-10 scale (1 the lowest and 10 the highest) rate yourself on your degree of self-discipline. In any area where you score lower than an 8, write down your thoughts about how exercising more self-discipline would impact your life and business if you moved that score up to a 10. Remember, self-discipline, just like success, is a choice.

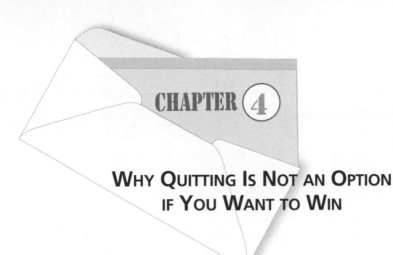

CHAPTER 4

WHY QUITTING IS NOT AN OPTION IF YOU WANT TO WIN

Here is a sad fact: Most people who come into the network marketing profession quit! There are many ways to view that statistic. Quitting is not unique to the network marketing industry. People quit school, they quit jobs, they quit marriages, they quit exercising; quitting is easy. By their nature, people often quit when the going gets tough. Deciding not to quit ensures that you are going to be way ahead of the masses. When you realize that you can be quite successful by sponsoring as few as 1, 2, 3, or 4 leaders, it just makes sense to persevere until these leaders show up.

Can you imagine going through life with a voice inside of you crying out that you are a quitter? What a terrible thing to think of yourself or of someone else. Those who choose to quit fail to persevere because they lack an expectation that they will discover what is missing that would result in the achievement of their goals.

The great orator Winston Churchill gave a graduation speech shortly after the Allies had vanquished Hitler.

Churchill's entire speech is said to have consisted of six words: "Never, never, never, never give up!" Churchill's admonition is both incredibly profound and undeniably true; quitting is *not* an option if you are going to win in life. Quitting is a disease that will grow out of proportion and smother accomplishment if it finds a host in which to live.

Virtually every day of your life you will hear an inner voice encouraging you to quit something. Quitting always represents the easy (but undesirable) road, the path of least resistance. This path leads to a lack of belief in yourself and in your ability to accomplish what you have conceived mentally and emotionally. The quitter's path of least resistance leads to doubt and disappointment. It is the path that ultimately leads to failure.

The path of least resistance destroys any potential for character, because it steers clear of those events that *must* occur in your life if you are ever to test your mettle, toughen your character, and temper your resolve. Each time you *embrace* challenge as a new opportunity to grow, you will become more and more disdainful of the path of least resistance. You will be too busy blazing the trail to your greatest potential to even think about quitting!

Imagine for a moment what kind of a place America would be if Martin Luther King Jr. had quit. Certainly, he faced moments when he felt as though he was making absolutely no progress in his quest for racial equality. Do you suppose there were times when he was tempted to forget about excellence and reset his personal default on average? Doing so would have meant selling out his vision and all the people who looked to him for inspiration and leadership.

What about the men at the Normandy beachhead who stepped off their landing craft into a murderous barrage of machine-gun fire? What if they had quit? Some of the men on Omaha Beach, horrified by the grim spectacle of their buddies being mowed down in wave after bloody wave, were tempted to give up. They huddled motionless in the sand, trying to present the smallest possible target to the lethally accurate Nazi gunners. Then a lieutenant stood up amidst the hail of gunfire and roared, "Are you going to lie there and die or get up and do something about it?" The men stood up and renewed the assault. Their commanding officer had helped them return to their commitment to excellence.

The pages of history are replete with tales of the great victories that were won by those who refused to quit and of the tragedies of unfulfilled potential from those who gave in and gave up. A refusal to give up and quit speaks to the depth of one's character. The history of network marketing is filled with great stories of victories that came from sheer determination and a refusal to quit. This same industry has as its heritage the tragedy of people who could have developed a great lifestyle if they just exhibited the character to stick out their pursuit of their dreams.

One of the greatest gifts that you can give yourself is the promise not to quit. Making the promise is one thing . . . fulfilling the promise is entirely another. You see, quitting is easy . . . it creates that instant gratification that we spoke of earlier. Quitting does not call on you to dig deep within yourself to test the measure of your character.

Consider the following scenario. Imagine that your mother and father have worked and sacrificed to save their hard-earned pennies all their lives. They have never lived in the house they probably could have afforded because they were saving their money to surprise you one day with a wonderful gift that would affect the rest of your life. They didn't go out to movies. They took only one or two vacations in the past 20 years because they were so dedicated to this gift they were going to present to you today. They sit you down and with tears in their eyes explain how much they love you. They say that they have worked very hard all their lives and have delayed gratification in many areas so that they could present you with this check. They hand you a check for two million dollars and tell you that they want you to buy your own business so that you can be the master of your own destiny. Now, imagine that to become a distributor for your company and take part in the income opportunity, it costs two million dollars, instead of the paltry amount that you actually paid to be affiliated with your company. With tears in your eyes, you thank your mom and dad for their generosity and promise that you will be successful in the building of your business. You promise you will not let them down.

In the previous scenario, how easy or difficult would it then be to quit? How would you treat your business under those circumstances? Would you hesitate to invest in your knowledge about the business and be reluctant to acquire the necessary leadership skills? Would there be any amount of rejection that would dissuade you from the mission of succeeding so that your parents' efforts and sacrifice were not in vain? We invite you to hold your network marketing business with this same great appreciation and value.

One of the great things about a network marketing business is that it doesn't cost much to become involved. One of the terrible things about a network marketing business is that it doesn't cost much to become involved. With such a low threshold of risk, it is easy for people to walk away if they are not immediately rolling in money.

By deciding early that quitting is not an option, you will have passed 85 percent of the people who come into this profession. That decision alone will put you in the top 15 percent of distributors who get started in the first place. As in life, just showing up every day to work your business with a great attitude is half of the battle. Decide very early in the game that quitting is an unacceptable response to adversity, rejection, and difficulty. Become a perpetual student of the network marketing game, committed to acquiring enough information and expertise to convince you that your ultimate success is inevitable.

If you are unwilling to go through the process of rejection, rise up above the daily difficulties, and experience the personal development necessary to become an attractive business partner and sponsor, then this business is not for you. You are likely going to be personally tested more in this business than with anything else you have ever done. Are you going to shy away from these challenges or embrace them, knowing that the struggles and defeats will turn you into the person you need to become to achieve success? Don't fear the process, embrace it. Embracing the process of becoming the person you wish to be will separate you from the masses of people who hope for a better tomorrow but are unwilling to pay the price necessary for success. Make yourself a promise. Quitting is not an option. Quitting is a pattern of behavior that is all too easy to repeat. Persevering is also a pattern of behavior that will repeat itself. Draw your personal line in the sand. Decide that with this journey, there is no such thing as quitting. It is simply not an option. When you make the firm decision that there are no events, no people, no disappointments that will bring you to the point of saying, "I quit," you will have given yourself permission to do whatever it takes to be successful.

CHAPTER 5

MAKING COMMITMENTS THAT COUNT

Our ultimate success or failure in our network marketing businesses (as well as in life in general) will stem directly from our commitments. Each moment of each day, network marketers can picture themselves at a fork in the road. They can choose to honor their commitments to themselves, their business, and their team or they can fall prey to taking the path of least resistance that dishonors their dreams and vision. They can choose to risk and offer their prospects the possibility of a life-changing opportunity or they can focus instead on being liked or looking good and keep silent. They can commit to being rigorous with their team members, from their commitment to their success, or they can opt to sell them out and avoid any uncomfortable situations. Everyone is committed to something. Those who build wealth and achieve personal and economic freedom choose commitment to actions that are in alignment with their vision for success.

If we were to break the concept of success into components, one component that is critical to your success is your willingness to make commitments that will pave a road to the ultimate attainment of your vision. If we were to study the daily habits of the world's most successful people, we would find that individuals who reach top levels of achievement make commitments to themselves and they *don't* break those commitments under any circumstances.

Just like attitude and self-discipline, the willingness to commit to a pattern of behavior that will impact your life in a positive way is a decision that has to take place in the head and in the heart. Successful marriages happen because both partners are committed to the relationship. Getting in shape results from a commitment to regular exercise and the maintenance of proper eating habits. Traditional business enterprises succeed because the owners of the businesses decide that they will commit sufficient time, money, and effort to create a winning business scenario.

In network marketing, winning is about making commitments to yourself to do what it will take to attract, train, and champion organizational leaders. It is also about setting an example that can be duplicated by your team. The following sections outline the commitments that you will want to make if you are going to be that inspirational leader, able to do those things that will lead to the successful building of your business.

LEARN ABOUT YOUR PRODUCT LINE

There is no greater way to learn about your product line than to use as many of your company's products as possible. In order to lead the way by setting the proper example in your organization, you must become an aggressive promoter of the products. Your company's products provide the foundation that makes the income opportunity possible. Extraordinary products are one of the things that differentiate legitimate network marketing companies from illegal pyramid schemes.

Remember, network marketing is a relationship business where the marketing campaign is conducted person to person fueled by word of mouth endorsements of the products. You will never be an effective advocate for the products if you do not personally use and derive benefits from your own product experiences. To enhance your personal experiences and credibility, experience as many of your company's products as you can. Obviously, there may be certain products that pertain to the opposite sex, to pets, or to special situations or conditions You'll need to learn to use the testimonials of others who are able to experience and witness the benefits of these products firsthand. For those products you can use, you will be well served to substitute and replace any competitive company's products with your own. Learn all about what differentiates your products and makes them special or unique. Develop as many aggressive uses as you can for your products to expand how they can be utilized and enjoyed. Become passionate about your products and share your love for them with others whenever you can.

LEARN ABOUT YOUR COMPANY AND ITS HERITAGE

Just about every established company in network marketing has a heritage of which their associates can be proud. Remember that successful network marketers become adept at telling the story of their company's origins, its products, and the opportunity that exists as the result of becoming an independent distributor of the products. Taking the time to know all about the company that you are working with will affect your ability to powerfully tell the story about what attracted you to it. A pride and loyalty needs to shine forth when you speak about the company to which you have pledged your partnership and entrusted your future. To the extent that you can embrace your company's culture and proudly speak of its evolution, you will be more effective in urging your prospect to consider joining you in partnership to create the company's bright future.

LEARN ABOUT YOUR BUSINESS AND COMPENSATION PLANS

Great leaders in network marketing don't depend upon someone else to show the business or explain the compensation plan for them. They commit to understanding their business plan, explaining what makes their company's compensation plan remarkable, and they become adept at supporting others to draft action plans of their own. They then spend their careers empowered by this knowledge as they passionately go about sharing how their company's plan is impacting their lives and those who join them in partnership.

As you get started, find someone in your upline who understands the dynamics of your plan and sit down with them to go over all of your plan's intricacies. That does not mean that you need to share all these intricacies of the plan with every one of your prospects. However, every once in a while you will run into someone who just has to know the full details of your plan before they can enroll or take action. When showing your plan, you will always want to keep it simple and basic, but it is great to have the intricacies tucked away in your head, just in case your prospect or new business partner wants to know more. After all, a true professional knows all aspects of their products and their business and compensation plan. One word of caution here: Don't freeze and delay action simply because you don't know all the intricacies in your early days. If you are new to the business, "I don't know" is a great answer to detailed questions, as long as it is followed by "I am working with some very knowledgeable people who will have the answers and I will get you the answer by tomorrow." That is what an upline is for: to get answers in your early days. Don't fall prey to paralysis of analysis. Just commit to learning about the plan in good time, so that you can eventually pass this knowledge on to others without requiring upline assistance.

LEARN ABOUT PEOPLE IN YOUR LINE OF SPONSORSHIP WHO HAVE SUCCEEDED

Everyone likes to hear stories about success. In whatever organization you are with, there are stories of people just like you (and very unlike you) who have decided to make commitments that changed the direction of their lives and the results they were experiencing. Those people got committed and won. They built network marketing organizations that created significant incomes that impacted their own lives and the lives of those people they introduced to their company. Spend time getting to learn the inspirational stories of these people. The more stories of success you are able to share, the more credible, relatable, and believable your business will appear to others. Find out who the top producers are, and make every effort to meet them personally. You might even offer to take them to lunch to get to know them better and to learn their story and any advice they might wish to share with you.

SHOW THE PLAN ENOUGH TIMES
TO CREATE MOMENTUM

If you are going to generate an expectation of success in your business, you must share your plan enough times each month to gain momentum. Network marketing industry statistics tell us that, as a leader, you will begin to gain momentum in showing your income opportunity a *minimum* of 15 times each month. That is the low bar on the leadership scale. Aggressive leaders typically commit to do whatever it takes to make at least 20 to 25 or more presentations each month with an appropriate follow-up meeting scheduled. Make a commitment about the minimum number of times you will share your income opportunity plan on a monthly basis and stick to it. Remember, if you would like to awake one day with 1,000 prospects introduced to your business on a daily basis, you must set the example of activity that inspires others and creates momentum in your business.

CREATE AN INFRASTRUCTURE OF
POSITIVE INFORMATION THAT WILL
HELP YOU BATTLE DISCOURAGEMENT

One of the facts about any type of network marketing or sales business is that you will get turned down by lots of people before you find those who see the value in your offering and agree to join you. You can decide to let these refusals serve as a means of discouragement or you can develop the mental toughness that makes you feel 10 feet tall and bulletproof, unaffected by any negativity you encounter.

Make a commitment to create an infrastructure of positive information in your life. Whether your information source is audio programs, books, or associations, you can't afford to be around anyone who drains energy from you. In life, you are what you think in your heart. Create an atmosphere of positive input that will create a protective barrier from any negativity in your life or business. To the extent that you expect that your success will be inevitable, you will be buoyed by an unshakable belief in yourself, positively motivated to do what it takes to achieve it.

WORK ON YOUR ATTITUDE EVERY DAY

A great attitude is a never-ending, day-by-day project. The world is full of people, events, and circumstances that can provide an excuse for maintaining a less than optimum attitude. Ultimately, remember, you are in the people business. People follow leaders with great attitudes. They don't follow those with bad attitudes or even fair attitudes. A great attitude under *all* circumstances is the sign of a great and inspirational leader.

Maintaining a great attitude takes work and commitment. It requires you to be continually aware of the need to remain positive, upbeat, and believing in the awesome future success for you and all who join you in implementing your plan. Leaders possessing superior attitudes become adept at creating empowering interpretations of any events, circumstances, or things that others say or do that would likely derail those with a lesser commitment to a sterling attitude. Know that all challenges and problems you will encounter as you build your network marketing dynasty will only make you stronger and wiser. Whenever the going gets tough, return to your vision for your ultimate success. Create an interpretation that supports you in realizing that these challenges are all for the good because they serve you in your personal development, making you wiser and stronger, and will make your eventual success all the sweeter.

REMIND YOURSELF EVERY DAY
WHY YOU ARE DOING
WHAT YOU ARE DOING

One of the main reasons people quit network marketing is that there is a disconnect between what they want (the thing that got them involved in the first place) and the daily work involved in building a successful business. It will serve your attitude, level of belief, and ultimate success to remind yourself every day why you initially made the decision to become involved in this business. What is your motivation? What is your vision about how your networking business will impact your life? What dreams will it make possible? What are you seeking to accomplish? Whose lives will you be contributing to with your success? Keeping a connection between these dreams and the activities required to manifest them takes commitment. It is a habit that can make the difference between being a dreamer and someone whose dreams come true through deliberate action.

PUT IN AT LEAST ONE YEAR
OF CONSISTENT EFFORT

Most people who quit network marketing do so because they lack the commitment to do whatever it takes for as long as it takes. Success in network marketing is not nearly as difficult if you are clear about the big picture. Keeping the right attitude and resolute commitments in place on the way to your success is the tough part. Get committed to do whatever it takes for one full year. Results will always take place when there is consistent effort for a long enough period of time. Consistent effort creates significant improvement in mastering the required skill sets. Mastering these skills increases results and leads to greater confidence and momentum in your business. The majority who quit their network marketing businesses do so within their first year, before they were able to identify and see the results from attracting at least one significant leader into their organizations. You will be amazed at what can happen with one year of committed, consistent effort. Commit to giving yourself the time necessary to find your first great leader.

PRIORITIZE TIME ON YOUR CALENDAR FOR YOUR BUSINESS

Most people do not have enough extra time for their network marketing businesses. They are far too busy with their jobs and with dealing with the challenges of daily life to participate in a second business. People who win the network marketing game simply make time on their calendars and make their business activities a consistent priority. Once they make the commitment on their calendars, they live by that commitment.

If you find yourself challenged by time availability, consider the fact that you have the same 24 hours today that anyone else does. Success is all about the priorities you set and the commitments that you make to see those priorities through. People often become frustrated with time management. It seems that there are never enough hours in the day to devote to work, family, friends, fun, and a new network marketing business. Successful networkers know that the answer lies in managing their commitments, rather than their time. Each day, list the actions you wish to accomplish for the next 24 hours. Prioritize your list, setting aside focused time for your family, job (if you still have one), and for your network marketing business. Be sure to mark off the hours you will devote to prospecting, and follow up each day. Without managing your commitment to speak with new prospects and follow up those who express an interest, you will be vulnerable to all the distractions life throws your way. Those who are not totally committed to structuring their days to move their businesses forward powerfully and on purpose will find that too often they will end up doing what is convenient instead.

CREATE A REWARD SYSTEM
FOR YOUR EFFORTS

The most successful network marketing professionals will tell you that they remain committed to rewarding themselves for hitting milestones on the way to their ultimate realization of personal and financial freedom. A reward serves as a personal recognition that you are on the way to fulfilling your mission. From time to time, everyone needs refreshing and a battery recharge along the way. Exhausting yourself on the way to winning is no fun. Get committed to take a breather and relax for a brief time when you hit milestones that signal success in moving forward toward your long-term goals.

Create a list of the rewards you will enjoy as you hit each milestone on your journey. Whether it is dinner at a special restaurant, a weekend away in the mountains, or taking a Caribbean cruise, it will support you to know that a fun reward awaits your hard work and efforts. However, beware that you do not fall into that all-too-common trap of stopping the type and level of action that got you to that accomplished company compensation plan rank or other milestone in the first place. It is important to set a time frame appropriate for your reward, and then recommit to resuming your plan that will take you to the next milestone on your journey.

ALLOW YOURSELF TO BE BAD
UNTIL YOU GET GOOD

Zig Ziglar has a wonderful saying: "Be willing to be bad until you get good." In the network marketing setting, that means not waiting until you know everything about your business model or products to get started. Whatever it is you need to learn, you will certainly get better by doing it. The best way to learn and the greatest teacher in network marketing is the sharpening stone of experience. Whatever the work task involved in your business, strive for excellence, but don't hold yourself to a standard of perfection. Perfection is pretty hard to duplicate and will only disempower those who cannot possibly live up to that impossible expectation level.

ATTEND ALL COMPANY AND
UPLINE SPONSORED EVENTS

With very few exceptions, every great leader in the network marketing world had their original fire fully lit at an event sponsored either by their upline organization or their company. A person's willingness to commit time and effort to prospecting and other necessary building activities is always determined by their belief level. Corporate and upline events serve to affect the belief levels of those who attend because they are as much about meeting successful leaders and hearing their stories as they are about training to build a large business. One significant outcome of attending a seminar is that many sitting in the audience for the first time had their belief levels dramatically raised by the event itself. They then take this elevated belief and share the fire with those they prospect and those they enroll. If you were to have the ability to interview the top network marketing producers, you would be amazed to learn the stories about how many leaders saw the light at an event.

Association in network marketing is a very powerful concept, particularly when you understand that your level of commitment about the need to attend events becomes the example for your organization. You can't expect your organization to attend and enthusiastically promote all impending events if you do not attend them and promote them aggressively yourself. We have yet to meet a top network marketing leader who has not used these events to his or her advantage. With the prevalence of long-distance sponsoring and building via telephone and the Internet, the events are often the chance for partners to meet face-to-face, develop deeper relationships, and take their businesses to an entirely new level. Commitment in this area will pay huge dividends.

CREATE A SOLID CUSTOMER BASE

How would you like to have 1,000 customers using (and often recommending) your products? This can be easy to do if you commit to developing 10 good customers yourself. By personally committing to the concept of creating and maintaining 10 good customers, you will be setting an example of commitment in this area. Your team will see this and follow your lead. When you have developed 100 distributors who are willing to follow your example and get 10 new customers each, you will have 1,000 customers in your business. This will create a solid foundation of product users that will likely lead to more customers being introduced to your products as well as some business builders who see the income opportunity after learning to love and appreciate the benefits of the products. Commitment to introduce customers to your products leads to proper duplication. The opposite is true as well. Your failure to attract customers will duplicate, resulting in diminished product usage throughout your organization.

FIND OUT WHAT YOUR DOWNLINE PARTNERS' DREAMS ARE AND SUPPORT THEM IN CLARIFYING POWERFUL, COMPELLING VISIONS FOR THEIR LIVES, ALL MADE POSSIBLE BY YOUR INCOME OPPORTUNITY

If you want to keep your people in the game and progressing in the building of their businesses, commit to finding out what they want and continue to keep their efforts connected to that vision. As a leader, the first step in this activity is being a good communicator and finding out what your people want. Take a sincere interest in your team members' dreams and make them part of your overall vision.

Everybody has a hot button that gets them motivated to do extraordinary things. All of your people are capable of accomplishing astonishing things if they are properly motivated to do what it takes to achieve them. The source of this motivation is expectation. If they expect to be successful, they will maintain a high level of action and do what it takes to realize these expectations. Clear and inspirational positive visions serve to fuel self-motivation and action.

Richard Brooke, network marketing visionary, tells us that we all already have a vision for our lives. If we look around us, it is this vision that is manifesting everywhere. If we do not like what we see taking place around us, we have the ability to substitute a new and inspirational vision instead of the current disappointing one. For us to replace the old vision with a new one that motivates us into action, we will need to gain clarity about every aspect of the vision. This includes what we'll have and where we'll live (and with whom) as well as what we'll do on a typical day at work or play. It also extends to include the qualities we'll be known for, the person we will *be*. We also will want to clarify who the people and organizations are to whom we will contribute when we have achieved the level of personal and financial freedom made possible through network marketing.

When we have a clear written vision that we read twice a day and believe in its inevitable accomplishment, we will be motivated to do those things that will support it. Likewise, if our vision for the future is negative, one in which we expect to fail, we will be motivated to take the easy way out, to not speak with enough people, and not speak powerfully when we do. After all, since we expect to fail anyway, why bother? We can then gloat about being right about expecting to fail and tell others "I told you so!"

Get committed to believing in your leaders and support them to keep their visions for success connected to their work activity. There is no stopping a human being who has a burning desire that they cannot live without. Your commitment to stoking their flame occasionally, by knowing what is emotionally important to their hearts, will support them to return to their motivating visions and to do what is often inconvenient or uncomfortable in order to make those visions a reality.

INVEST IN YOURSELF IN THE AREAS OF PERSONAL DEVELOPMENT, LEADERSHIP DEVELOPMENT, APPEARANCE (TEETH, HAIR, CLOTHES), AND IN THE TOOLS OF THE BUSINESS

Successful network marketing leaders don't skimp when it comes to their businesses. They commit time, effort, and money to make their businesses a success. If you are going to win big in network marketing, you must commit to investing in yourself. You are your business's engine, the heartbeat of your business, and its greatest asset. You have to be willing to invest in building a better, more effective *you* from the inside out and the outside in. From physical appearance to mental preparedness, you are worth committing to in money and time.

All network marketers would do well to take on an effective personal development program. Your business will likely grow to the degree you are able to develop strong, empowering relationships with your team. Such relationships will be served by developing your listening and communications skills. Your business will grow more rapidly to the extent that you are effective in coaching and championing your team to success. Train yourself to continually look for what's working well in your conversations, actions, and business partnerships and for what's missing that, if put into place, would support you to be more effective with others and more productive in your business. For a self-study personal development program designed for network marketers, check out *10 Weeks to Network Marketing Success CD or Cassette Album plus Workbook* by Joe Rubino.

Consistent commitment to the right principles will create

a foundation for massive success. Imagine how your total commitment in the areas just discussed would affect your business. Now imagine that commitment level being duplicated 1,000 times. How about 10,000 times? It is doable, but it all starts with you. You are now and will always be the example of commitment for your organization. Get committed!

CHAPTER 6

THE POWER OF A COMPELLING DREAM THAT DRIVES YOUR DAILY ACTIVITY

We get what we expect. If we expect to be successful in our network marketing businesses, we will take on the task of becoming educated in conducting our new profession with skillful effectiveness. Success in network marketing is partly a numbers game. If we begin with the unrealistic expectation that we can just speak with a few people and then sit back and watch as they go on to build for us a huge organization, we are likely fooling ourselves. Out of every 100 people, a certain percentage will join our businesses, if we take responsibility for creating sufficient value with our presentations. Out of this group, a certain percentage will step into leadership and go on to build a network marketing dynasty. Once we track our results and compute our success ratios, it's then simply a matter of speaking with enough people to put the odds of finding a leader in our favor.

Of course, if we immerse ourselves in personal development, we will also continually research how we can be more effective in our communication, create more value for our prospects, and better support our team members to duplicate our success. Personal development, by its very nature, is a process that takes time. Beginning networkers would do well to take the pressure off themselves by realizing they are novices and will develop the skills that successful networkers possess over time. This expectation of constant and never-ending improvement, coupled with a commitment to hit the numbers, by speaking with enough people consistently and persistently, will support new networkers by getting started on the right track in business.

Effective massive action drives the growth of network marketing organizations. To sustain this necessary level of action requires self-motivation. Self-motivated leaders do what is necessary to achieve success. Motivation is sourced by expectation. When we expect to win, we do the actions needed to bring about this expectation. Our expectation comes from our vision of how we see ourselves progressing in our businesses and how we envision our lives being impacted by our income opportunity. In other words, it all begins with the dream.

The power of a dream or vision for your life is one of the essential keys to winning in your network marketing opportunity and to winning in life. People who can wake up in the morning with a burning desire in their hearts to accomplish their dreams will blow past people who wake up in the morning seeking only the next week's paycheck.

People will subject themselves to the stress and discomfort of what is new and challenging *if* there is a big enough reason. This general rule is magnified when your reason is tied to your heart, that is, when the reason is a reflection of those most important values that just demand to be honored. Don't ever get in the way of a man or a woman who is in the emotional, passionate pursuit of a dream that they cannot live without. You'll get run over!

If you are committed to living a life infused with passion and free of regrets, you will change your life's paradigm based on the fact that you have a dream that is so compelling and so important to your heart and soul that you become unstoppable while in the pursuit of this dream. Perhaps you can't imagine changing your life or feeling that a dream is so compelling that you must pursue it. This simply means that you have not yet connected with your life purpose, that extreme motivation that will nourish your soul and make each day so worth living that you can't wait to get at it.

Remember, people's lives will move when you introduce them to your potentially life-changing opportunity. A person's life is like a train engine heading down the track with an enormous amount of power and momentum. To change the direction of something that powerful, there must be a huge reason and an enormous amount of force applied. People will not muster that amount of force unless they have a dream for a different scenario that is so compelling that they just can't live without it.

If you can get to the point where your daily activity has such compelling purpose by being tied to the accomplishment of your dream, your effort and your results will be transformed. If you can learn to help other people tie their daily activities to the desires of their hearts, you'll win by developing on-fire leaders!

Success doesn't always come easily, no matter how badly you may want to realize your vision for your life and business. Let's say you want to become a trial lawyer and have mentally and emotionally connected that life's vision to your heart. What if you took the LSAT and received the same score as a monkey with a pen? Do you quit, even though that vision has become a white-hot passion inside of you? To be successful, the pursuit of that vision must become the defining purpose for your daily activity. If you truly have passion in your heart to pursue a dream, a seemingly insurmountable thing like a monkey-man score on the LSAT cannot deter you. If you are only invested in the idea of becoming a lawyer on an intellectual level, you will probably give up. However, if the burning desire deep in your heart is to become a lawyer, you will sign up for classes, read every book, and retake the LSAT as many times as it takes. You simply cannot abandon a dream for which you have that much passion. Obstacles and disappointments will happen. The fact that you hit a roadblock does not define you. How you react to the roadblock, however, does. How you handle the pursuit of your dream establishes a behavioral template that will shape every other pursuit in your life. Will you cut and run at the first sign of serious opposition? Or will you regroup and push ahead? Connect to that dream, whatever it is, with every fiber of your being. Fulfilling your dream is a way of life. Becoming emotionally connected to your dreams and goals is a characteristic that will separate you from the crowd throughout your adult life. The man who possessed the burning desire to become a trial lawyer understood that, and John Terhune went on to become one of the most successful trial lawyers in Florida.

You will meet a great many people who are trying to achieve goals, but who have not tied the desires of their hearts to the activity they are about to undertake! They just don't yet possess the right mental attitude to be effective. Consider the example of the couch potato who was out of shape and overweight. We all know someone (or perhaps many others) just like him. He didn't exercise and seldom watched what he ate. About once every six months, he would announce that he was beginning a new diet, which generally lasted about two weeks or less. Then one day, he went for that long overdue physical, and the doctor said, "We are checking you into the hospital *right now*. Your arteries are 80 percent blocked, and you are just days away from a massive heart attack." He was wheeled into surgery, and doctors performed a quadruple-bypass procedure. Before he was discharged from the hospital, the doctor told him, "If you want to live, you have to change your lifestyle *immediately*. You must eat differently, begin an exercise regimen, and start paying more attention to your health."

Six months later, this former out-of-shape walking timebomb is lean and fit. In place of the baggy sweat shirts he wore to conceal his fat, he now wears sleek running apparel because he has transformed into such a fitness fanatic and these clothes represent who he has become in this new lifestyle. He has seen the light. It took coming right to the edge, with death waiting just over the next hill, but he got in shape for the first time in his life and stayed that way. The close brush with death gave him a reason that was *compelling* enough to do something that he had not previously been motivated to do. It wasn't that he was incapable of getting in shape before the surgery, and he understood, intellectually, that his flabby condition was a health risk. However, he wasn't emotionally motivated to shape up until he had been given a compelling reason!

Your willingness to sacrifice and invest at a *much* higher level increases dramatically when your goal is emotionally charged. When you pursue anything with passion, you will *always* surpass the results you'd get by only engaging with intellect alone. If you emotionally connect to your goal, you will dig down into your soul to find the bedrock of resolve that makes all accomplishment practically inevitable. You will drive straight through roadblocks like discouragement, rejection, physical exhaustion, and any discomfort caused by personal discipline and delayed gratification. Motivation driven by emotion is the irresistible force that will bulldoze any object that is blocking your path to success.

If your goal is to reach the top levels of achievement in your network marketing opportunity, throw yourself emotionally into that pursuit. You'll have to harness the power of your heart to accomplish the task. When you are determined to reach your objectives, no matter what challenges appear, you'll tap into an awesome inner power that you may not have even previously realized that you possessed. It is your ability to throw your heart over the bar that will make the difference.

Here are some very clear consequences of having a compelling dream:

- Your tolerance level for temporary setbacks will increase dramatically if you are propelled by a dream that is heartfelt.
- You will send out an invisible message to people you speak with about your opportunity that you are going somewhere in life. Your energy will scream "I am on the path to great success and if you join me, you can be successful, too!" People like to be a part of a winning team. If you are showing the opportunity without the passion that naturally flows when you are chasing a dream, people are not going to catch the fever of a man or woman who is so inspired.
- Having a dream will make investments in your business, in yourself, and in your personal development a natural consequence of your pursuit.

You'll want to invest in things like the following six categories:

1. Self-development books, tapes, courses, and personal coaching
2. Dressing for success with clothes to look the part
3. Necessary functional and optional cosmetic dental work
4. Enhancements to your general physical appearance
5. Tools to build your business
6. A travel budget

Go touch things that motivate you and represent your dream. Visit that house by the ocean and test drive that brand new BMW 750 il. Making your vision and all it encompasses real will re-ignite you and energize your daily activity. Get to know what is important to your leaders. Listen to them and find out what their dreams and aspirations are. Get involved in the emotional pursuit of helping your team accomplish their dreams. Bring your team members brochures that represent or help stimulate their dreams. If you help enough other people get what they want out of life, you will get everything that you want. This is the true power of network marketing. Rarely will you ever have the opportunity to create the same quality of bond that happens when you actually put forth effort, sweat, and investment in the passionate pursuit of someone else's dreams and they accomplish them.

When you show your prospects your income opportunity, the secret to sparking their motivation and achieving enrollment success is being able to create a connection between their wants and the opportunity you're presenting as the vehicle to realize those desires. Speak from your heart to theirs, and watch what an emotional connection can do to propel people forward in passionate pursuit of their dreams.

CHAPTER 7

STARTING YOUR BUSINESS WITH THE RIGHT EXPECTATIONS

As you will learn throughout this chapter, the tools that empower someone to reach their full potential rarely consist of just a talent or skill. More often than not, the tools that empower a person to reach his full potential have everything to do with the way that he thinks. As we have heard from so many wise philosophers over the years "as a man thinketh, so is he." If you have ever doubted that statement even a little, this chapter should put any doubt forever to rest.

To become a success in network marketing requires an attitude that reflects a heartfelt *expectation* that you will succeed, no matter what, not a hope or a wish that it might happen. You must know in the depths of your heart with absolute certainty that becoming a top producer will soon be a reality for you. There must be no doubt in your conviction or in your belief. For such doubt will both translate into something being missing that will keep your prospects away and sabotage your success in countless insidious ways.

To really get the vital nature of bringing this attitude of positive expectation to your pursuit of network marketing success, let's talk for just a minute about how your mental state of mind affects the physical behavior that must accompany the pursuit of any great ambition. Consider the following mental picture as a powerful reminder of the importance of getting your thoughts right. Have you ever seen a martial artist break many bricks, cement blocks, boards, or blocks of ice with only the force from a blow from the hand? One blow and over a dozen large ice blocks that are stacked on top of each other break cleanly. It is a very impressive sight. These martial artists will tell you that the physical feat is only possible when it is prefaced with the right mind-set. Martial artists must clearly see and expect in their hearts and minds' eyes to break through the blocks long before they strike the blocks with their fists. There is a transfer of belief from their minds and hearts into the physical actions that they take to break the blocks. Without the pure transfer of expectation that their fists will go through the massive amount of ice, there is no way that they could accomplish such a feat. Timidity, fear, or a lack of total conviction will translate to less force. The mental state must precede and become the foundation for the physical execution of the act.

Attitude is a state of mind that reflects the feelings of your heart. When emotions are compelling, they can translate into actions that have the power to shape and define your reality. When actions lack the foundation of expectation, the results they produce are comparable to rolling a pair of dice; that is, they are unpredictable and can't be counted upon. Without actions founded in conviction and the type of commitment that always produces the best results over time, we are forced to simply hope that what we desire will happen. What is missing is the powerful force that turns expectations into manifestations. Expectation is the reflection of a belief in your heart that is transmitted to your brain. Knowing that a certain result is inevitable becomes the foundation for your actions. Victories don't just happen. They are the manifestation of an attitude of expectation combined with a massive amount of effort, thus overwhelming the possibility of failure and resulting in success. It all starts with expectation because this anticipation of success changes the behavior put forth, thus resulting in the manifestation of a self-fulfilling prophecy. Expectation precedes the massive, focused, and effective activity that separates you from the crowd in network marketing and in life.

Now that you realize that you must approach your vision quest of becoming a megasuccess in your network marketing pursuits with a completely convicted mind-set that reflects a genuine expectation that you are going to win, let's examine the underlying dynamics required to bring this attitude of expectation to your life. Let's start by analyzing what factors must be present in your life to support a reasonable expectation of becoming wealthy from the pursuit of a network marketing business. The single biggest factor that will support your vision quest is a great self-image. I am not talking about arrogance or being falsely prideful or cocky about who you are and where you are going. It is not about being stuck on yourself. Rather, a soaring self-image translates as an inner feeling about who you are, a deep-seated self-respect, that gives you a confident posture and an inner sense that you can accomplish anything that you put your mind to if you want it badly enough. It's about knowing in your heart that when you put your mind to something, you are unstoppable. It's also about being proud of who you are based on the sum total of your interactions with other people, your application of self-discipline that separates you from the average person, your stick-to-it-ive-ness, integrity level, the care that you express for others, and the general sense that you are an extraordinary individual because of the life path you have chosen. High self-esteem translates into a genuine self-respect for the person you have decided to be.

The stronger your self-image, the greater is the likelihood that you will approach your network marketing business with an attitude that shouts out, "I expect to win." The louder and more genuinely that the inner voice can make that statement, the more that your actions will reflect that statement of expectation and the more others will be drawn to your energy.

The presence or lack of a genuine expectation of success in your network marketing quest will produce predictable consequences in your life as well. Let's take a moment to look at what will result if you do not do what is necessary to achieve success in your business with a genuine expectation of winning. First, without such an expectation, you will grow tired easily. Anything yielding great results will take great effort. Winning in network marketing is never easy and without challenges. Generating stellar results will require great effort. There will be times when your hard work seemingly produces no results at the moment. If you are not confident that you will ultimately win big by following your action plan, exhaustion will likely set in quickly. In contrast, when we *know* we are going to win, we are resilient, do not tire easily, and expect that our continuing efforts will soon be productive. Winning always starts in our heads!

Failure to take on this task with an expectation of a victory will cause you to become frustrated with the process. Because network marketing is always about dealing with people, it can be very frustrating at times. The way that you deal with people and your level of patience you show them will be greatly affected by whether you know that it will all be worth it. If you expect to be successful and have made the decision to do whatever it takes to make that happen, then dealing with these temporary frustrations will be a far more manageable task.

If you don't expect your victory to be inevitable, you will find yourself coming up with great reasons to quit when the going gets tough. You will justify your failure by pointing the finger at everyone—except yourself. Justification and blame come easily when an expectation of success is lacking.

Without the right expectation, it will be nearly impossible to bring great people to your game. How high you fly in this business has everything to do with *who* is on your team. Building a network marketing organization is exactly like a sporting event. You can have the greatest game plan in the world. Still, you won't win unless the right players are on the field. If you perform in a way that gives others great confidence, they will see you as the type of leader worth following. They will need to see that you *are* successful and if they will join you, *they* too can share in that same success. Successful people like to win and they like to associate with people who are on their way to winning. The only way to project that air of impending victory is to believe in your heart that it is assured.

Networking leaders possess an attitude of expectation regarding their future success that inspires others to take action well beyond what they would ever do on their own. A large part of your success will depend on your ability to reach the hearts and souls of people by the example you set. If your attitude does not scream out that you believe you are going to win, you will fail to inspire others to reach *their* full potential. This inspiration can mean the difference between having others join you with a passionate expectation to achieve their dreams or having them pass on your opportunity because it did not excite them.

Great things will follow your positive expectation because it will impact your daily habits. Belief in your ultimate victory will have you dealing with adversity and failures as an event instead of a destiny. You will be able to operate empowered by the fumes of faith instead of the fuel of results. You will consistently attract great people to your game because they will feel your resolve and commitment and want to be part of your winning team. When your energy is sourced by a positive expectation of success, it will attract others like a magnet.

NASA taught us a great lesson about expectation during the space race of the 1960s. President Kennedy understood that the United States was losing the race into space and what would ultimately be the race for technology. In a political address, he boldly announced that the United States was going to land a man on the moon before the end of the decade. Now, to understand the magnitude of this statement, one must realize that the technology to go to the moon was not yet in place as he made that statement. Fortunately, NASA did not set their expectations based on what was possible at that time. They *decided* that they were going to the moon. They *expected* to go to the moon by the end of the decade. They proved that when the goal is compelling enough and when one is driven by an attitude of expectation, nothing is impossible. The fact that the technology wasn't there when they made the decision to go for it had nothing to do with the effort and heart that they put behind the project. They knew that they would figure out the technology on the way there *if* they had an expectation that they would find a way. This belief drove the physical activity that resulted in this incredible victory for humankind. Had they been tentative in their belief and not expected a victory, they would not have made it happen. The same dynamics hold true for us as network marketers in pursuit of our dreams.

So what if you don't currently possess the type of self-image that allows you to know in your heart that you are going to win in network marketing? What can you do to develop that attitude? Here is a short list of what you could be doing from this day forward specific to developing a genuine, heartfelt expectation in your victory. First, decide to put the past behind you and refuse to let any disempowering evidence deter you in achieving your goals. The past need not equal the future if you do not expect that it will. Build your self-image one day at a time. A self-image is a cumulative view of how you see yourself responding to life's challenges. Today, you have a choice about what you do and the way you go through life. Decide now to make choices you will be proud of, choices that honor your declaration about who you say you are. This declaration is an exercise based on courage. You get to invent the type of person you will be from this moment forward. Transforming who you were to who you are now only requires recognizing, in each moment, your ability to choose. Once you understand that you can act minute by minute in choice, you then simply take responsibility for making decisions that honor the person you have decided to be. Doing so will impact every aspect of your life, from your personal relationships to your work ethic, to the degree of self-discipline you exert daily. As you strengthen the muscle of honoring your commitments rather than what is convenient to do, you will feel better and better about the person you are. The more that you trust yourself to act in a way that honors your values, the more you will feel that you deserve to win and the easier it will be to act out of these expectations by doing the things consistent with being victorious.

Your greatest progress will result from working moment by moment on your attitude. Your attitude results from the decisions you make. Begin the habit of measuring your attitude every day (1 being terrible to 10 being a great attitude all day long). Rating yourself daily will cause you to focus on improving your attitude and this intention will transform your results.

Read the works of people who have achieved success. It will become apparent to you that people who win expect to do so. Their mental state dictates the amount and duration of their physical effort. From athletes to politicians to business leaders, an expectation of victory is the foundational thought process common to all people who win big.

Realize that your success is a process that will have good days and bad days. No one who has ever won big in life and certainly in network marketing has had an easy, challenge-free ride to their victory. Success is a process. By embracing the process and all the challenges that come with it, victory will be more readily attainable.

A great rule to take into your journey to network marketing success is that people will live up or down to your expectation of them. This same dynamic happens within each of us as well. You will live up or down to your expectation of yourself. Make the decision to become unstoppable. Expect excellence and a massive victory and watch it manifest before your very eyes!

PART TWO

MASTERING THE CRITICAL SKILLS

CHAPTER 8

CREATING LEADERS

O ur network marketing incomes will grow in relation to how many leaders we are successful in identifying and developing. In answer to the eternal question, "Are leaders born or made?" the answer is actually both. A select percentage of children grow up in nurturing families that champion their self-esteem, and as a result of a combination of genetics and environment, they emerge into charismatic and effective leaders. Unfortunately, this is most often not the case. What about the rest of us then? The good news is that anyone who decides to declare themselves to be a leader gets to act from that declaration from that minute onward, operating from a decision to lead and do whatever it is that leaders do (have and articulate a compelling vision, inspire others to embrace a vision, and step into action in order to realize it).

Here's a rhetorical question for you to think about. This may be the most important question for you to consider specific to your network marketing business because it will set your mission and dictate your activities. What business are you in? The answer to that question might seem terribly obvious, but here is a story that will make you stop and think for a minute or more, and will most likely hit you like a cooler of ice water thrown over your head.

The following story illustrates the importance of having the right answer to this question. The late Peter Drucker was recognized as the top management consultant in the entire world. He taught, wrote, and was paid a great deal of money to help companies tweak their business models. Peter Drucker was asked to come in and consult for a company called Service Master. Now, you may know that Service Master is an organization offering franchise opportunities. The franchisees actually go out to people and deliver a great product and/or service to homeowners. They may run a pesticide business or they may do cleaning. There are many different aspects of Service Master, but the bottom line is that by flying under the Service Master flag, you are recognized as someone who is going to deliver a very high quality product to homeowners in the United States. Peter Drucker went in to do a consultation with this company and he asked them the question, "What business are you in?" Now if you know anything about Service Master, the answer to that question might seem obvious. Most would say that their business involves going out and providing a great service to people who are homeowners in the United States. Actually, at the end of a couple of days, Drucker suggested that this was *not* the business that Service Master was in. The business Service Master was in was actually going out and finding, recruiting, and training really great people who will then go out and deliver the products and services. It turns out that the products and services that Service Master is known for are actually byproducts of the business that they are actually in. This business is really about going out and finding, recruiting, and training really great people.

Like Service Master, you are in the business of finding, recruiting, and training great leaders! One of the reasons that many network marketing organizations have not exploded to comprise massive numbers is that too many people think they can take the easy path. Please get this straight right now. Easy is not good when it comes to building a network marketing business. For the vast majority, having an easy time of it is inconsistent with the indisputable laws of the universe. It makes no sense to think that making a lot of money should be easy. Network marketing is simple, but not easy. If it were terribly easy to build a million dollar plus business, everyone would have already done it and there would be no extraordinary opportunity remaining for those not already involved. Those people who have fallen for the false hype of automatic downline building systems and programs where minimal effort is required with promises of quick wealth will rapidly learn this harsh reality.

Network marketing is not easy because it involves dealing with people. Any time you are dealing with people, you are going to have challenges. The soul of network marketing is in the relationships between the people that comprise the essence of the business. Though you may attract a prospect on the Internet, you will still need to build the relationship in person or on the telephone. Those who will make a lot of money in network marketing today and in the future are the people who are willing to build community and leadership within their organizations. That is not an easy job. However, how easy is it to go to work every day for 30 to 40 years or more?

Our microwave society and get-rich-quick mentality seeks the path of least resistance. In life and in the business world, easy is usually inconsistent with long-term success. You are going to have to pay a price for success anywhere you go. It is the law of nature. If you don't pay the price for success and build leadership, then there is no way an organization will last over the course of decades or longer. The people who come in and promote network marketing as an easy get-rich-quick-without-paying-the-price business give the profession a bad name. Because of this sort of false hype, people come in and soon become disillusioned when they realize that network marketing is a vocation that requires the mastering of a necessary skill set and one that follows an effective, duplicable system (see *The 7-Step System to Building a $1,000,000 Network Marketing Dynasty* by Joe Rubino for one such system), to earn the really big incomes that most desire. Your determination dictates your mission and the things you must do to accomplish the mission.

The following philosophy can help you be incredibly successful in network marketing. If you are going to build a long-term business that will allow you to live the lifestyle you are seeking, you will never succeed unless you build a leadership base that will develop other self-motivated, self-sufficient leaders who will, in turn, spawn other self-motivated, self-sufficient leaders within your organization. Short of doing this, you are going to be in a constant state of replacing people. You will be running a babysitting service that will drain you of energy and sour you on the potential for your business's ultimate level of success. If you ever run into anyone who left network marketing because of burnout, it is because they never took the time to realize the enormous difference between doing something for someone else and empowering them to lead and create leaders within their organization.

Building leaders is not an easy, quick thing, but it is the most rewarding task we can take on to build our dynasties. It requires being effective in dealing with people. It doesn't happen overnight, but it is a process that requires stretching people to expand outside their comfort zones as they boldly risk and do the things that leaders do. Developing leaders requires that you invest your time and effort in these people over time. Leadership demands that you must be willing to involve yourself in this process of championing others to be their best. While building leaders and working with people is not always easy, it can be tremendously rewarding. There will be few moments in life that will give you a higher high than seeing someone you've invested in win their victory and gain financial freedom themselves. If you are looking to build a huge organization and claim the personal and financial freedom that is there for you through the vehicle of network marketing, be prepared to put yourself in a personal-development program that supports you to expand who you are so that you will better be able to support others to step into leadership and do the same, following your example.

Although the concept is a simple one, so many people fall into the trap of not taking the time to build leaders. You will learn in this chapter how to speed up the process of developing leaders by empowering people with the tools to become leaders. That means you don't have to do all of the leading in your organization. You need to understand the difference between pulling the proverbial cart by yourself, or having a team of leaders help you push the cart to your collective victory.

Let's look at the quest to build a megasuccessful network marketing business in terms of the following metaphor. Ending up with the type of long-term, residual income that you don't have to work harder to maintain than you did to build is analogous to getting a big wagon, like the type used to give hayrides, up a steep hill. Get that picture in your head. When you succeed in getting the wagon to the top of the hill, you ring the bell, and financial and personal freedom are yours! Imagine that every time you enroll someone into your business, they climb into this big wagon that you must get to the top of the hill, if you are going to reach the top levels of your opportunity. If all you do is sponsor them and they get in the wagon but they never get out to help push, there will come a time when the wagon gets too heavy. In this scenario, you just might decide that building a business is too much work and not worth the struggle because the wagon gets heavier every time you get someone in the business. But what if you could develop a process in which your new recruits start out in the wagon, but eventually they get out and help you push the thing up the hill? That is what you are looking for—people climbing out of the wagon and taking on leadership roles in the team effort.

The only way to make this happen within your organization is to create the expectation with your new people early on in their experience that their days of catching a free ride in the wagon with someone else pulling them are limited. If you implement nothing else from this book, please take this information and apply it to your business. You may be one of those people who will do whatever it takes (prospecting, following up, training, coaching, etc.) for everyone else if they can't or refuse to do these actions themselves. Although that may be effective in the beginning, it's completely unrealistic in the long term as your organization grows. Every time you do something for them that they could be learning to do for themselves, you are depriving them of the chance to acquire the skills they will need to succeed. You may think that they can't show the plan as well as you can, they aren't as good at follow-up as you are, they aren't as good at getting people started as you are, and so on. When you feel that way about your associates, it won't be long before you resent them, and they resent you. The sooner you realize that you are cheating those people out of the opportunity to grow into a leadership role and to stand on their own two feet, the more successful you will be. When you realize that, you will truly know what business you are in. You are in the business of finding and training great leaders, who will be excited, not frightened, to take the leadership reins in their own hands before passing these same reins onto the leaders they too will develop. This realization may change what you tell people as they are looking at your business opportunity, and, very importantly, it will change the expectations of those people considering your business opportunity.

Your message may now sound a lot like this: "Just get in, I will do everything for you. You use the products, but I will help you make the phone calls and show the business plans. You won't have to do any of that." You might even be afraid that they won't get in if you don't do the work for them. Hopefully, by now, the light is starting to flicker on inside your head. It's not about sticking them in the wagon and dragging them up the hill; it is about letting them sit in the wagon, knowing they soon need to learn how to help push the wagon up the hill. In other words, transition your thinking from the intention of just getting people into your business so you can win, to helping people get into their *own* businesses so they can win. Transition your business to empowering your leaders to develop the skill sets and confidence that will allow them to run and grow their own businesses, attracting others to them. Rather than trying to be the engine that takes your success train to the Promised Land, instead decide to be just one of the cylinders in the engine.

Critical Lesson: *You will have a much more successful*

*network marketing organization if you take the time to train 10
leaders, than if you just attract 1,000 followers.*

By building leaders, you will also be able to enjoy life
without needing to have a phone stuck in your ear 20 hours a
day, 6 days a week. The 1,000 followers who are not serious
about taking leadership roles will wear you out, unless you
have 10 leaders in place to help support the followers. Those
who refuse to take on personal development and refuse to do
what leaders do are the cause for burnout among people who
have the work ethic to build a big organization but try to do it
all on their own charisma and efforts. There is a time for
training and supporting your new associates by doing three-
way calls and sponsoring interviews with those associates.
There is also a time for them to leave the nest and be capable
of doing the same exercises with their new associates. It is one
thing to build a group of followers, it is altogether another to
build a group of leaders.

Let's now look at the kinds of changes you can expect
when you decide to build leaders.

- You'll focus most of your efforts on targeting those people
  you deem to be leadership material. You'll go after those
  with prior histories of success in other areas. You'll look
  for people who are charismatic and who are good communicators. Start concentrating on people who know how
  to pay the price for success, and who understand principles of success like sacrifice, personal self-discipline, and
  delayed gratification.
  □ This is not to say that anyone can't reinvent them-
    selves and declare themselves a leader without any
    prior evidence to substantiate this declaration. We
    will always challenge people to take the next step in

the development process and we will work with those who demonstrate a willingness to be coached and to do those exercises necessary to be successful in this business.

❑ This is also not a justification for you to prejudge people. It is sometimes those you least expect to be great in this business who surprise us all and go on to build huge network marketing dynasties. Prospect everyone as the opportunity arises, but devote your concentrated efforts to going after those possessing the qualities you value in your business partners. Challenge everyone to take the next step as you coach each in the process of doing what it takes to be successful. Work with those who make the effort and leave the door open for those not ready to do so, without being attached to the hope that they ever will be ready.

■ Start creating an expectation in each new person that there is a window of time that you will term *training time*. This introductory period can typically last anywhere between two and six weeks. Challenge your new associate to take on more and more responsibility as this time period progresses. This is the time to train, coach, and challenge your new partner so that he or she can make the transition from trainee to leader-in-training, and eventually to leader.

■ Assure them that you have an effective duplicable training system (*The 7-Step System to Building a $1,000,000 Network Marketing Dynasty*) that will empower them to grow and maintain their own business momentum with or without your support. Be sure they know that you are serving them much better by empowering them to develop the skills necessary to run their own businesses rather than if you did all the work for them. By doing this, you are creating a template for their businesses that will translate into independence for them in several ways. Ultimately, it is important because this is the template that you are going to set in place for them so their own businesses will be filled with leaders who they won't have to baby-sit. If you do it all for them, their future and the success they reach is totally up to you, not them. It's only fair for them to be the captains of their own destiny. You will teach them how to pilot and navigate the ship and you will always be there to assist in their journey. However, there will come a time when you will expect them to become totally self-sufficient leaders who inspire others to join the team and subsequently pass along the baton of leadership to others.

□ Realize that if your message scares them, perhaps you have the wrong person. Work with those willing to take direction and move their businesses in a forward direction by honoring the requests you make of them.

■ Create an expectation early in the process that they are going to be leaders. In fact, encourage them to declare that they *are* already leaders just because they say so. Once they own this title, they will simply step into a leadership role at every opportunity they will then create deliberately. People will live up or down to your expectation. Hold others as capable, competent, powerful, and successful and they will respond to your challenges by manifesting these qualities. If you set the bar too low and interact with people who feel they are not capable of ever being self-directed and stepping into leadership, it can dramatically affect the quality of people coming into your organization. By holding others as incompetent, helpless, stupid, or lazy, you will just as likely manifest these qualities in the people who show up around you.

□ Although this message tends to scare some people off, you will begin to grow faster because the people who do come in will tend to stay in the wagon for only a short period. Then they will get out, help push the wagon, and carry their own weight, as you all charge up the hill together.

- Decide to maintain a posture that says "I'd welcome the opportunity to have you join our team in partnership, and if you do, I will commit to your success to the same degree that you commit to your own, as displayed by your actions. Though I'd love to have you join us, I am not attached to having you or anyone else do so. There are plenty of self-motivated people who are willing to do what it takes to be successful in our business, so there's no need to be desperate in attracting those unwilling to do their part in working toward their own success." This posture is welcoming and invites everyone to consider if this business may be for them, but it never is needy in approaching potential partners. Create a screening process based on this philosophy for your team and then teach this screening process to your people. It has to do with how they hold their value and the value of their partnership in supporting others to be successful in business.

- Have *The Talk* with your organization. *The Talk* can help define your posture for prospecting and attracting those ready to take responsibility for their own success. Let your people know that you are only looking for serious business people who will dedicate time, effort, and money to help win in their own businesses. Essentially, tell them to focus on attracting sharp, hardworking, self-motivated, and committed people.

- Endeavor to get to the point where you are turning people away who do not meet your criteria as partners. Invite them to become customers or to enroll so they can purchase product at wholesale cost, which will allow them to dabble on their own until they are willing to make a true commitment to their own success. Communicate these options to those you sense unwilling to treat this opportunity like a serious, worthy business. By turning them into a wholesale customer, you can communicate that you value them and will take care of them, but you will spend the majority of your time, which is limited and valuable, in developing your leaders who truly understand the opportunity you've offered them.

- Make them realize *you* have the cookie. You have the knowledge and the understanding to help them develop a successful business enterprise, but they have to pull their own weight if they are to earn your partnership commitment. They must be willing to devote time on a consistent basis to making a list, contacting and inviting, showing the business opportunity, investing in the tools of the business, attending events, and learning the business. Get them to realize from the beginning that the ultimate success or failure of their business is their responsibility. Of course, you will always be willing to help them push their wagon, but you simply won't push it for them forever.

Adopt the following six-step process for training someone to be a leader of their own business, and they will most assuredly be able to duplicate the results themselves.

STAGE 1: DO IT
FOR THEM CORRECTLY

You do the task (whether it is the phone call, assisting in making the list, showing the plan, or doing the follow-up) to show them the right way to do it. As a general rule, you should probably do each task they will need to see and learn to do themselves 6 to 10 times. Liken it to driving a boat. Occasionally, you look at the other person who has never driven the boat and say, "Would you like to try it now?" During this time, you have ample opportunity to talk to them about product use, product sales, their dreams and ambitions. It is a great bonding time. People who try to build a network marketing business without investing the time and effort to get to know who their people are and what they want in life are wasting their time. Success in this business comes from championing others to realize their dreams. You can't do this if you don't know what your leaders' dreams are!

STAGE 2: LET THEM DO IT WITH
YOU TO SUPERVISE WHAT
THEY ARE DOING AND HOW WELL
THEY ARE DOING IT

Have the associate do the task with you present (on the phone or in person when feasible) so you can watch them and assist them in developing the necessary distinctions so they can eventually do it powerfully themselves. You can make the tweaks necessary to help them do it most effectively and support them to gain confidence about what they are doing.

STAGE 3: THEY DO IT ON THEIR OWN AND DEBRIEF WITH YOU

Turn each behavior your new associate will need to master over to them after a period of coaching on each activity. This supports them to gain momentum in the activity and to learn to become self-sufficient. After they experience doing the behavior, you work with them to examine what worked well and what was missing that, if put into place, would make the next time more effective.

STAGE 4: HELP THE PERSON YOU TRAINED TRAIN SOMEONE ELSE

Since success in this business comes with duplication, make sure your new associates are following the examples you set during their initial training phase to develop leaders in their own organizations. Again, always support them to identify what worked well and what was missing to make the next time more effective and productive.

STAGE 5: GET THEM INVOLVED IN A LEADERSHIP DEVELOPMENT PROGRAM

Developing leaders is a process, and you cannot and should not want to try to do it on your own. However, continuity of message and continuity of development are important ingredients in creating the concept of duplication. Of course, if you are going to lead and train leaders, you will need to be a leader yourself, modeling the type of activities you wish them to adopt. If you are going to be the role model that your people will look up to in your business and are willing to follow, you must make a conscious decision that you are going to read more books, listen to more content, maintain a better attitude, and exude more expectation of victory than anyone else in your group. True leadership comes as a result of setting an inspirational example of the right principles that make the business grow.

STAGE 6: BECOME THEIR FRIEND, CHEERLEADER, CONFIDANT, AND BUSINESS PARTNER

Inherent in building leaders within your organization is creating relationships with those leaders. Great relationships and friendships are at the center of long-term successful business relationships.

- Empower each of your team members with the ability to be the leader of their own organizations.
- Recognize them for their accomplishments with cards, flowers, dinner, or some other sort of acknowledgment.
- Allow them to be center stage without stealing their well-deserved recognition and time in the spotlight. One of the greatest gifts a leader can give to another leader he or she supported in developing is to eventually fade in prominence by allowing the new leader to take center stage. You will only benefit by championing your leaders to become more effective, productive, and powerful than you are.
- Get to know them—birthdays, anniversaries, children, and so forth. Send them a congratulatory note or a small gift to remind them about how much you care.

- Know their dreams—bring brochures and catalogs of what they want—homes, cars, vacations, and so on.
- Spend time with them and have fun with them. Get used to playing and creating happy memories with them.
- Help them set goals that keep them moving forward. Hold them as greater than they hold themselves and challenge them by making powerful requests that are in *their* best interest to move closer to achieving their dreams.
- Set regular strategy and debriefing times that mix business and pleasure.
- Remember, you are creating a community and these people are the leaders of the community.

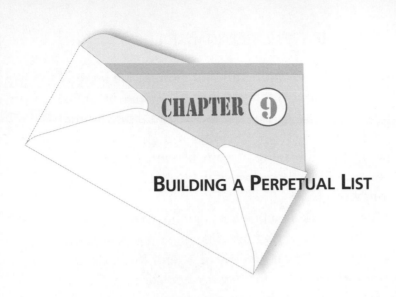

CHAPTER 9

BUILDING A PERPETUAL LIST

struggling network marketers have one thing in common. They lack an endless source of prospects to speak with on a daily basis. One of the secrets to effective prospecting is to assume a posture of confidence and nonattachment to any prospect needing to get into the business. There must be no desperation in the prospector's voice and the energy put forth must never be needy or based on a fear of scarcity of prospects. By having an endless source of prospects awaiting, networkers can confidently know that, if their income opportunity is not right for the current person, there are always many others waiting in the wings that they will move on to speak with next. This skill is one of the most important things you can teach your people to set the stage for a strong and productive business. Teaching your new associates this skill properly is truly like handing them the keys to the kingdom.

The first skill to learn and duplicate involves building a list of people with whom you can share your opportunity, and then turning the list from a finite number of names to an infinite file of prospects with which you can share your business opportunity. Let's start at the point of being brand new in the business opportunity. Being a beginner will give you the purest perspective on the value of your list and it will highlight how the list is one of the most valuable assets in any network marketing business.

First, because you are in a business that has to do with duplication, you will have to bring other people onto your team and support them to develop other leaders and to create the amount of volume necessary for *them* to realize their financial dreams. By focusing on their success, not yours, you will make money in your business opportunity. In the beginning, when your team consists of only you, you can only create a very limited product volume from your own personal consumption and whatever retail sales you generate. Even if you aggressively sell your company's products, the sales you can generate from these efforts are going to be limited to what you can do individually. If you want the lifestyle that potentially awaits you by duplicating your efforts through a large network of people who do what you do, you are going to have to share the networking concept with other people. Many will become your product customers and many will go on to develop a network marketing organization. Either way, you have to expose the income opportunity and products to others. The best way to begin this process is to create a list of people.

Begin to create your list by recording the names of everyone you know without initially ruling anyone out by prejudging them. This does not necessarily mean that you are going to show your business plan to everyone on the list. It is nonetheless important to create the full list to include everyone you know or know of, so that your new person can visually see the art of list finesse. So how do you build that initial list? Pretend someone will hand you $10 for every name up to the first 100 people. After 100 people, someone will hand you $50 for each name up to 200. From 200 onward, someone will hand you $100 for each name thereafter. Outline this same scenario with every new person you will support in getting started. As you are about to see, this is a very purposeful exercise meant to teach an important success concept to your team members. By supporting your people in the process of building their lists, you will be helping them to understand what business they are really in. Understanding this concept defines what your mission is and what the mission of your new people will be, specific to the list you have just created.

This will be the first of many opportunities to remind yourself of the answer to the all-important question "What business am I in?" If you are truly in the business of building leaders who are going to help you push the cart we previously described up the hill to the top, you are going to sort through this list with a definitive purpose.

Allow me to explain further by offering another analogy. Consider standing in front of a busy thoroughfare that sees a lot of traffic go by on a daily basis. Imagine if you stopped every car that went by to show each person in every car your business plan with no screening process to separate the people who are willing to be coached to follow a successful model from those lacking the traits necessary to be successful in this business—traits like belief, commitment, work ethic, personal effectiveness, etc. Imagine, too, that some of the people lacking these essential traits actually got in and you had to dedicate your own hard work and effort in helping them build a network—though they showed no openness to being coached to follow a successful business building methodology. There would be no telling who might come by and get into your business or if they even possess the willingness to develop those traits about success habits and self-discipline that will lead to success in network marketing or in any other venture. To sign up just anyone and everyone without regard to their willingness to learn and implement the things required to achieve success in this business would be an example of no filtering process being exercised on your list.

Here's a second extreme example to illustrate the point. Imagine you only stopped the cars of those people who had already achieved great levels of success in life. These people have paid their dues and earned success in other endeavors. They know about business principles like investment and delayed gratification, and they know that success in a business does not come overnight and that, sometimes, it requires several years of consistent and persistent effort. Now, if you only showed the plan to these people, your ratio of getting people in would perhaps be lower than if you allowed everyone to sign up (depending on the economic times), but your focus and your ability to more effectively build leaders who would take the responsibility for building their businesses would be transformed.

But what about those individuals who may have no prior history of success but who are willing to follow your company's success system, who are open to your coaching, and who are willing to make a commitment to personal development and to action? Of course, you will support them in their quest to achieve success through the vehicle of network marketing. It's analogous to a chess game. You make a move and they make a move. As long as they are willing to follow your lead, become trained, establish a continuing action plan, and create a structure for personal development whereby they take on learning the distinctions required to become better communicators; more effective in their prospecting, enrollment, and training skills; and remain open to feedback and coaching, they would make worthy partners.

The most productive strategy is to go after those who have shown a history of success in some other arena and leave the door open for those willing to do what it takes to be successful in building a network marketing business. This will require that you set your business up to champion those willing to accept responsibility for their own success. It also will mean letting go of those who display no commitment to being coached, no commitment to action, and an unrealistic dependency on you to build their businesses for them, rather than with them. In other words, some leaders will show up with a history of qualities for success that they have displayed in other areas. On the other hand, some will lack prior success histories but will be willing to declare themselves to be leaders and do what leaders do in building their network marketing businesses.

With the mission of finding, sponsoring, and developing leaders, identify people on the list that already possess the qualities that you would expect successful people to share in common. Start with people on the list whom you would like to have on the board of directors of your very successful company. Invite them to explore a fit for your income opportunity first. Next, go after those you are not quite so sure about because they either lack a successful prior history or you are not as familiar with what their accomplishments have been or what their aptitude for success will be. Rather than rule anyone out whom you are unsure about, present them with your opportunity, clearly spelling out what traits you are looking for in the partners you take on (a willingness to craft a vision for their success in the business, an expectation of doing what it takes to realize this vision, a commitment to following through on a detailed action plan, a willingness to work with you to put any missing elements in place as you work your plan in partnership, etc.).

There is an important point to make here. You will not always know who is ready or right for your business. Some, whom you think should be perfect for your business, may not see a fit for their lives. Others, without a clear record of success elsewhere, may be willing to now do what is necessary. As long as they are willing to be coached to do those things required to achieve success in this business, you will be willing to champion them in partnership to make their success happen. Some may not know what they initially want. They may come in as a customer, or get off to a slow start as a mere participant. Some of those people are going to transition from riding on the wagon and, eventually, they will jump off the wagon and become leaders. Keep the invitation open for them to accept the challenge and take the next step in the evolution to leadership, but don't let them drain your energy by not following through on their promises or expecting you to build their businesses for them because, after all, you are in the business of building leaders. Welcome those people and pay attention to them, always offering them the opportunity to step into a more committed role. But spend 80 percent of your time with those who come in as builders and walk their talk by supporting their words with action.

In short, first go after the leaders who have demonstrated that they possess the qualities successful people display. Then, go after those who are willing to be coached and who have the potential to take on an eventual leadership role. Pass on those who clearly demonstrate a reluctance to follow direction or a refusal to accept responsibility for their own success.

Here are some rules for prioritizing your list to identify your potential board of directors:

- Whoever someone is before they get into the business is a great predictor of who they will likely be in your business. People can change, but it is time-consuming and they should demonstrate a willingness to do so backed by action.
- The most successful people will treat you with respect even if they say no. They will be the quickest to congratulate your vision and success, and oftentimes, if they don't get involved, they will point you to other people who will get involved. Successful people know that success is a journey, and they respect anyone with the courage to embark on the journey.
- Successful people associate with successful people. Even if they don't become involved, they may know someone who is an extraordinary prospect who may well become a great leader in your organization. Always remember to ask for referrals, even if your prospect may not see a personal fit at the current time. We like to say something like "Sally, I understand that our business may not be right for you at this time. Would you be willing to share with me the names of at least three sharp people you know who might be willing to take a look, knowing that I will always respect your referral with no pressure or obligation?"

If you are sponsoring the people with proper success attitudes and traits, when they go through the exercise of building their initial lists, and then identifying those whom they would like to have on their board of directors, these people are likely to sponsor three to six business builders into their organizations. The original list that your new people develop with your assistance should yield a number of business builders to get their organization going. Because it only takes three to six good leaders to build a huge group that will lead to financial freedom, the importance of getting each of your new partners off to a fast start cannot be overemphasized.

By supporting your new partners to get off to a good start, setting the right expectations for leadership, and helping them learn the skill sets necessary to build their businesses, a much higher percentage of those people who engage will succeed. However, there will always be some who will not see the program through and will not grow into the leadership role you had hoped for them. Because of this, you'll want to become proficient at having an endless supply of names to continually add to your perpetually growing list. So, let's look at what you can do to be sure that you always have plenty of people to show the plan, to grow your business at will.

BUILDING A PERPETUAL LIST IS BASED ON ATTITUDE

To build a list that will never stop growing requires the right mind-set. By making a decision to go into what we call a *constant meeting mode*, you will ensure the long-term success of your business. This does not mean you will need to go down the street and meet everyone you see and shake their hands like a politician in search of votes, or go to malls and stalk sharp-looking people. However, it does mean that you are going to kick into a purposed, positive state of mind while setting your personal default on living a gregarious, outgoing lifestyle where you smile a lot and send off a positive attitude everywhere you go. By adopting a positive, high energy, expecting-great-results attitude, you meet more people every day and many of these people will be attracted to your energy and open to exploring the possibility of joining you in your business. People can sense when you are positive minded and open to creating a win-win scenario. Create and maintain a master prospect list, and carry a small pocket-size notebook in which you can constantly add to the list. If you are a happy person who smiles at people, says hello to people in a genuine way, and exhibits a positive, upbeat attitude about life, you will draw people to you. Conversations will be easy, learning people's names will be an art you excel at. You will go through life in a constant state of meeting new people and making new friends. A happy energetic person who has a good attitude and who smiles at other people will never run out of names of potential prospects because his list will be continually expanding. Network marketers who run out of names on their potential prospect lists have not made maintaining their lists a priority. By making your list a priority, you will be in the constant state of meeting people and adding them to your ever-expanding list.

It is important to remember that the purpose of your names list is to get people *off* your list. Imagine that someone made the following deal with you: They are willing to hire you and pay you $1,000 per day to do the following. You have to go to breakfast, live your normal life, and be happy, smiling, and outgoing to all the people you meet in the course of living your life. All you have to do is to engage one person per day whom you do not know in a five-minute conversation about nothing in particular—just friendly conversation in which you introduce yourself and learn the person's name and something pertinent about them. Could you do it for $1,000 per day? Sure you could. It would be a piece of cake. Well, to have a continuously growing list, that is exactly what you have to do. Put your people skills to work and meet people everywhere you go as you live your normal life. Remember, you can just as easily meet successful, confident people who have a greater chance of succeeding in your business as you can indigent, angry people who expect the world owes them a living. Take on the goal of purposely meeting people who represent a target-rich environment of sharp business and success-oriented people.

Over time, you will double and then triple the number of people you now know as your circle of contacts and influence continues to expand. If you have a physical list that is always growing, you will always have an inventory of people who are potentially in the looking zone. Maintain your master names list in a safe location, but always carry a small pocket-size notebook to be in a state of constantly adding to the list.

Here are some great general rules about adding to your list:

- Get into the habit of asking for peoples' business cards. Attend local business related meetings like Rotary, Kiwanis, the Chamber of Commerce, or other organizations where business-oriented people gather. Attend leadership conferences in your area. Get around the movers and shakers of your community.
- Put yourself in a position to meet people who are leaders. If you want to find someone who can hit a 500-foot home run, you won't look for such a slugger at a playground where young children are playing.
- Learn to be a great listener. Ask open-ended questions about people such as: What do you do for a living? How long have you been in that field? Isn't that a very hot field right now? Is that field affected by the economy like my field is? What got you into that type of work in the first place? Sounds to me like you still have a passion for it, is

that so? I have a son who is thinking about going into that field. If I sat you down with him, based on your experiences, would you tell him to pursue it or head into another direction? Learn how to ask a series of questions that lead your prospects to opening up the conversation in the area you wish to talk about. Show genuine interest in the other person and her business. If people are polite and if they have people skills, they will ask you about your interests and your business, providing you with the opportunity to share what you do with them, and you can gauge their interest in learning more about it.

- Learn the concept of dropping bread crumbs over your shoulder versus shoving the loaf of bread down their throats. It's all about developing your people skills and becoming adept at making friends.
- Learn how to build relationships with people before you talk about your business and thrust it upon them prematurely. By first focusing on building the relationship, you can allow for the time to provide the opportunity to talk about your business venture.
- Listen for phrases such as "I want," "I need," and "I wish I could" as people are talking. Pay attention to their passions and how much time they have to pursue them. Put yourself in the flow of sharp, energetic businesspeople, and take an interest in getting into their worlds.
- Never exclude someone because you think they are going to say no. Some of the most successful leaders in this business are people who most others were afraid to approach because others mistakenly assumed that they would never get into an opportunity like this.
- Make each negative response a potential addition to your list by asking for referrals of people who may be interested in their own business opportunity.

Note: For additional lead-generating techniques such as classified and display advertising, direct mail, home parties, professional business receptions, targeting niche-markets, generating leads via the Internet, purchasing opportunity-seeker names, and so forth, please see the following books by Dr. Joe Rubino where these topics are covered in great detail:

- *The 7-Step System to Building a $1,000,000 Network Marketing Dynasty*
- *The Ultimate Guide to Network Marketing*
- *Secrets of Building a Million-Dollar Network Marketing Organization from a Guy Who's Been There Done That and Shows You How You Can Do It Too!*
- *10 Weeks to Network Marketing Success: The Secrets to Launching Your Very Own Million-Dollar Organization in a 10-Week Business-Building and Personal-Development Self-Study Course*

CHAPTER 10

LIST FINESSE

There are really only five things that network marketers need to do extremely well.

1. *Create a list.* Be in the state of constantly adding new people to your list to show the business opportunity.

2. *Get good at contacting and inviting.* Once you've got them on the list, you've got to have the ability to give them a call or talk to them in person and get them to take the time to look at your business opportunity.

3. *Present your business opportunity in a professional manner.* You want to be able to show people the business plan and have them excited about what they saw. You've got to be able to show the plan in an effective way.

4. *Follow up.* This is a skill that people really fail miserably at. They show the business concept and then they don't get back with the people for three to five weeks, and the person who was excited during the presentation has completely lost this excitement.

5. *Get someone started properly.* Your new associates are ready to go. They have said they want to get in and get going. Now what do you do at this point to get them started properly?

Those who are interested in building a huge network marketing business are going to have to duplicate themselves through other like-minded ambitious people. The first stage in duplication is the creation of the names list. As beginning networkers contact others on their list, one of three things is going to happen. Number one, they are going to say, "No, thanks," or number two, they are going to become a customer, or number three, they are actually going to get involved with the intention of building a business.

We teach people to initially build the longest list possible including everyone they know. Do we want to show everybody on the list the business plan? Well, in lieu of what we've just said about developing leaders, the answer to that is no. When we first started our businesses, the answer would probably have been yes. If your prospects had a pulse and could sit there long enough without falling asleep, you would have shown them your business plan.

Because my time in life is short, I'd prefer to stack the deck in my favor. If my intention is to put people on my board of directors, I find it helpful to analyze who these people are (and the success principles they understand) before they are considered for the business. After all, why not speak with the sharpest ones first? Ultimately, I don't need 100 on my front line; I need only three to five really good ones that understand the game. If I find three to five good ones, through the process of duplication, we can turn these leaders into tens or hundreds of thousands of people over time. Becoming a friendly person who treats others with class will ensure having a continuous list. Running out of a list is a matter of mind-set. Having a perpetual list is also a matter of mind-set. It's all about the attitude that you bring to this skill.

As you continue to learn about investing the time to create a great list, also learn the important subtle difference between the act of making the list and who you are going to talk to first on that list and when.

An important dynamic happens when you put the names of everyone you know on your list. It involves both the physical act of adding someone to your list and the process of actually maintaining an always-growing names list. If you get into this habit of maintaining a list and keeping a copy of either the entire list with you (or some list that you eventually add to your master list), you will develop a habit of writing everyone's name you come up with on your list. Guaranteed, you are going to meet approximately 200 new people next year, and if you carry a list with you, there is a good chance that their names will be added to it. This effectively puts them in the queue to receive a call from you about your great products and phenomenal income opportunity. So it is important to put everyone on the list and add to it all the time. However, that does not mean that you'll necessarily want to speak to everyone on your list. Just because you know someone doesn't qualify them to become a serious potential customer or associate. Rest assured that there are people on your list who you don't want in your business. They may be negative or a pain to be around. They may be dishonest. They may have a terrible reputation that is justified. They may be the type of person who will drain you of energy or emotion. You might be wondering why you would even put them on your list. That's easy; everyone goes on the list, without prejudging them initially. The physical act of having and maintaining a list of *everyone* you know now, or meet in the future, creates a success habit that says that *everyone* goes on the list. Then, you play list finesse and start screening them according to your experiences with them and what you know about them. Some will make good customers. Others will warrant an invitation to take a look at your business. As you view this list, ask, "Would I like to have this person as a customer or as a partner in building a business in my company?" Remember, you only need three to six successful business builders to lock in a great six-figure income—if they are the right ones.

Here is a great rule to live by that will assist you in drafting the right team. Whoever someone is before they get into your business is likely to be exactly who they are going to be after they get into your business. Everyone has developed a habit set in his or her life that is blatantly obvious. You can easily recognize these habits if you know the person fairly well. People tell you who they are by their actions. If they are lazy, undisciplined, negative, or lack ambition before they go on your list, putting them onto your list doesn't change who they are. If they are enterprising, ambitious, self-disciplined, self-motivated, and a good people person with a great attitude before you put them onto your list, that is exactly who they are going to be should they end up in your business. Many people who quit network marketing simply get exhausted trying to drag the wrong person down the path of success.

Here are 10 questions to ask about a prospect when you are exercising list finesse:

1. Have they been successful in some arena before? Successful people have developed habits that previously have

led to their success in the first place. They will bring those same commendable habits into your business.

2. Do they enjoy interacting with people? Network marketing is a people business. The better the person's people skills, the greater their likelihood for success in network marketing.
3. Have they demonstrated an ability to work enthusiastically today with an expectation of receiving their reward tomorrow?
4. Does the person have other people following them? Are they centers of influence?
5. Are they fun to be around?
6. Is the person someone who vocalizes dreams, goals, or ambitions?
7. Does this person project a sense of confidence and the feeling that they are going places?
8. Is the person a go-getter and self-motivated?
9. Would you like to have this person on the board of directors of your company?
10. Would you be comfortable introducing them to the most important people in your life?

Remember, a potential prospect for distributor status can always become a prospect for customer status if they don't become a distributor.

Here are five questions to ask about a potential customer, especially if your product line supports health and wellness:

1. Is this person clearly proactive about exercise and their personal well-being?
2. Does this person seem to have a passion for health and fitness related products?

3. Does this person currently take products designed to optimize their health?
4. Does this person have any clear health issues that our products can address?
5. Would your company's products be a fit for this person?

All potential business opportunity prospects and potential product/service customers have the potential to lead you to other successful business builders if you remember to ask for referrals.

CHAPTER 11

NETWORK MARKETING IS A CONTACT SPORT

f a football player went into a game afraid of getting tackled, how effective a player would he be? Obviously, not at all! All too often, people make the decision to become involved in network marketing and proceed to go out into the world and speak with people about their products, income opportunity, and company. And guess what happens? Others don't see the value they did, or they think they are too busy, or they mistakenly confuse your potentially life-changing opportunity with a sleazy, pyramid scheme, or any other number of reasons that translate into them not being interested. The neophyte networker confuses this response with rejection, interpreting that it is the networker whom the prospect is rejecting. Perhaps, the novice networker takes this interpretation of rejection one step further, reasoning that "no one wants to do this." With such a faulty interpretation seeming to be true, it is no wonder why quitting becomes a sensible option! A hit or two and they're out, incapable of playing the game effectively.

CREATING A GREAT INITIAL SCRIPT (THE PITCH)

It is vital for you to create a succinct, clear, purposed verbal pitch that projects confidence in yourself and your opportunity. This pitch is designed to help you set up a follow-up phone call or meeting to share the business opportunity with your prospect. This pitch must be internalized so that it comes across authentically, not stilted or phony. It is spoken from the heart in such a way that your prospect does not know it is a canned speech.

In the investment world, this is referred to as an elevator pitch, meaning that you have as much time as it takes to ride the elevator up with a venture capitalist to convince them of the value in listening further. Once the elevator ride is over, so is your opportunity to make your pitch unless you have got your potential prospect's attention during the elevator ride.

Here are several examples of effective elevator pitches.

First scenario, for when you know the person and he or she lives close by:

> Tom, this is John. Do you have three to five minutes? I am running between meetings but had something I needed to call you about. The last time we had lunch, you were talking about how hard you were working and how little time you had with your family. I have been thinking about that ever since. I think I have come up with a solution. I can't promise anything but I think there is some potential here to solve your time-vs.-effort problem. We can talk about it over lunch. What is a good day for you, Wednesday or Thursday?

Now, let's examine this pitch sentence by sentence to explain the elements you will need to integrate into your pitch.

> Do you have three to five minutes? I am running between meetings but had something I needed to call you about.

If your prospect is local to you, you are purposefully setting up a scenario where you will not have time to go into the details of the pitch over the phone. You are being respectful of the possibility that they are busy at the moment and at the same time letting them know that whatever you have called them for won't take long. You must be respectful of the fact that people are very busy today.

> The last time we had lunch you were talking about how hard you were working and how little time you had with your family. I have been thinking about that ever since. I think I have come up with a solution.

You have recognized a need and have proposed that you may have a solution to the prospect's need. This is very important because you are coming to the prospect with a solution to something that is obviously important to him or her. You are showing sincere concern and wish to offer something that will contribute to the prospect's life and solve a problem. The prospect has reason to listen.

> I can't promise anything, but I think there is some potential here to solve your time-vs.-effort problem.

You have maintained your posture by not seeming overly anxious to the point of being willing to take the problem away from him or her. You have left the prospect with a possibility, but he or she has to take action if you are to explore the possibilities further.

> We can talk about it over lunch. What is a good day for you, Wednesday or Thursday?

You have presumptively framed the answer to your question by not asking the prospect if he or she wants to get together.

Remember, you are sure this will help solve the prospect's problem, so you are operating under the assumption that the prospect wants to deal with this issue. You don't ask if the prospect wants to get together; that is a given in your mind. It is not a matter of whether; it is a matter of when.

Second scenario for when you don't know the person and they live close by:

> Hi, Tom, my name is John. How are you today? Tom, let me get right to the purpose of my call because I know you are very busy. I am a businessperson. My business is to help busy people have more time for themselves while increasing their earnings. My flagship product is a proven system that can help anyone add significantly to their income while gaining more time for themselves. I would like to spend 15 minutes with you to explain our system with no obligation from you other than the time that you spend to listen to what I have to say."

Now, let's examine this pitch.

> Hi, Tom, my name is John. How are you today?

People do business with people they like and those who come across as competent in their delivery. Don't be afraid to get into some initial friendly conversation that will break the ice. The key here is don't go too far with this. They need to know that you are friendly and competent, but that will take less than one minute if you are confident in your tone and approach.

> Tom, let me get right to the purpose of my call because I know you are very busy.

Busy people appreciate you getting to the point but getting there in a friendly manner. Get to the point, but let them take a moment to like you on the way to the point.

> I am a businessperson. My business is to help busy people have more time for themselves while increasing their earnings. My flagship product is a proven system that can help anyone add significantly to their income while gaining more time for themselves.

Be clear and succinct describing what you do; less than 50 words will do. You must be very clear in describing the benefit that you can provide if they go beyond this call.

> I would like to spend 15 minutes with you to explain our system with no obligation to you other than the time that you spend to listen to what I have to say.

There's no pressure here and the person knows they will be able to learn about this system that holds benefit for them in less than 15 minutes.

Third scenario for when you don't know the person and they live out of town beyond meeting distance:

> Hi, Tom, my name is John. How are you today? Tom, let me get right to the purpose of my call because I know you are very busy. I am a businessperson. My business is to help busy people have more time for themselves while increasing their earnings. My flagship product is a proven system that can help anyone add significantly to their income while gaining more time for themselves. I would like to set up a call to spend 15 minutes with you by phone so that my business partner and I can explain our system with no obligation from you other than the time that you spend to listen to what we have to say.

In this scenario, meeting face-to-face is not an option. You'll want to schedule another time for the call to give it the importance it deserves. By having your prospect agree to set up a definite time, you are conveying the notion that the call will warrant a special appointment being set. You also have successfully persuaded your prospect to agree to setting this time aside, so you have created an expectation that the information you will convey will be valuable. By scheduling the three-way call with your business partner, you are also showing your prospect that you work as a team. You will later stress that the prospect will also not be required to conduct these presentations alone until they are competent to do so.

These are simply examples. You will want to get with someone who is very successful in your business, usually an upline mentor or partner, and get his or her help in creating a great elevator pitch to use when initially calling the prospect.

Here are five components of a successful elevator pitch:

1. The introduction: Confidently introduce yourself. If you have a name that is not a common name spell it out for them.
2. Get to the point to show that you respect their time and yours.
3. Make your initial pitch no more than 50 words. Brevity, clarity, and focus are key.
4. Offer a compelling benefit that will be likely to generate your prospect's interest.
5. Specify the fact that you will need only 15 minutes to explain your proposal.

In the elevator pitch, always include the most compelling benefits that are likely to appeal to the person listening. Always err on the side of brevity and never try to show your plan in your first phone call to the prospect. This will support you in maintaining an attractive posture, and it will send a message that your plan is worthy of your prospect's attention.

Remember, the mission of the call is not to explain the concept; the mission of the call is to secure a meeting (or follow-up call if not local) with the prospect so that you can present your business plan in a setting or at a time conducive to making a business decision.

Listen attentively and learn to respond appropriately to what your prospect says, guiding the conversation in a forward manner while responding to your prospect's concerns and questions.

(Note: For the five steps to effectively guiding a powerful prospecting conversation, see *The 7-Step System to Building a $1,000,000 Network Marketing Dynasty* and *10 Weeks to Network Marketing Success* CD Series, both by Joe Rubino.)

One of the biggest problems people have when making a pitch or presentation is that they don't listen to the questions or answers being given by the prospect. Imagine a trial lawyer who is so tied to his script that he doesn't listen to the answer of the witness. The lawyer begins, "Mr. Witness, where do you live?" Witness: "I live in Florida and I killed the victim by stabbing her 50 times." Lawyer: "And how long have you been living in Florida?" Listen to the answer you are getting and respond specifically to that answer.

Learn how to think on your feet. "Thinking on your feet" has to do with preparation and anticipation of questions or responses that you will get from the prospect, much as you did when you were a kid and you tried to frame in your mind an answer to the question you knew you were going to get from your parents.

Perhaps, in your work experience, you may have imagined a conversation with your boss before it took place.

Maybe you were going in to request a raise and tried to determine answers to your boss' objections in order to help you to get that raise. By running through the questions before you entered his office, you prepared for what may come your way.

You must take the time to do exactly the same thing before you make your calls. You must mentally put yourself in the conversation long before actually having the conversation. By doing this, you will be able to anticipate the questions, objections, or attempted quick dismissal to your pitch by the prospect. The more conversations you have, the easier it will be to anticipate your prospect's questions, concerns, and objections. It is a great feeling to be able to effectively listen through an objection or question that you have anticipated ahead of time and have your prospect respond positively to the manner in which you have honored their concern, embraced their objection, and offered a new way to look at the situation.

(Note: For a thorough discussion regarding the fine art of how to effectively listen through objections, see Chapter 8 of *Secrets of Building a Million-Dollar Network Marketing Organization from a Guy Who's Been There Done That and Shows You How You Can Do It Too!*)

With a little practice and experience, you can anticipate many of your prospect's questions and objections and be ready to effectively respond to them. It won't take long before you realize there are only so many questions and concerns that will ever be generated by your prospects in response to your pitch. This is where your role playing and practice are so vital. If you role play with someone before you make the calls, you can make a list of possible responses and frame answers to the responses that when delivered sound very smooth and unrehearsed. Anticipate the concerns your prospects will likely have before you encounter them so that you will be prepared to listen to them. Never argue with them! By doing so, you will only drive their objection deeper. Role play so that anything that your prospects ask you will have an answer that exudes confidence and competence.

Take the time now to complete the following very important exercise. Write out your pitch as well as some likely responses to questions, concerns, and objections that your prospects will likely have for you. Do your best to anticipate both your responses and what their potential replies will be to those responses.

First, a quick review of the six rules of the pitch:

1. The mission of the initial pitch is not to show them the plan; the mission is to set up a meeting or a follow-up phone call at a mutually agreed time and place.
2. Limit the amount of time through your brief, clear, and focused words.
3. Identify the benefit(s) to your prospects.
4. Assume they will want to schedule the meeting or call and will be interested in learning about your business proposal.
5. Give them a choice of meeting times.
6. Prepare yourself with responses to anticipated question or objections.

In summary, here are some questions and preparation points to consider before making your pitch:

My "Why" or Reason for Being Involved in This Business Is:

_____

_____

_____

My Mission for This Phone Call Is:

_____

_____

_____

My Pitch Is:

_____

_____

_____

First Anticipated Response:

_____

_____

_____

My Response to Anticipated Response 1:

_____

_____

_____

Second Anticipated Response:

_____

_____

_____

My Response to Response 2:

_____

_____

_____

Third Anticipated Response:

_____

_____

_____

My Response to Response 3:

_____

_____

_____

POSTURE

It is critically important during your phone contact with your prospect that you have an air of confidence and speak enthusiastically without sounding out of control. There is an important difference between projecting a confident, authentic, and enthusiastic demeanor and an overexaggerated, slick, and hype-filled pitch that will turn your prospects off. Some people naturally possess the authentic, believable, and confident posture that will have prospects sit up and take notice. This is clearly an advantage, but you can have the same advantage with practice and as the result of introducing the opportunity to someone of that stature.

The Successful Posture Equation
Posture = Total belief in yourself + Total belief in
your business opportunity + A good, authentic
elevator pitch delivered with enthusiasm

THE RIGHT PHYSICAL ENVIRONMENT TO MAKE YOUR CALLS

Let's focus now on an important element to support your personal power and effectiveness as you make your calls. There are good environments and bad environments in which to conduct your calls. Does your environment have kids screaming, dogs barking, or the TV blasting? All these will convey the impression that you lack professionalism and success. Your physical environment can have a great deal to do with how you come across on the telephone. Remember, you are looking to stack the deck in every way that you can to create a scenario that leads to success.

Recently, long-time radio host Paul Harvey was commenting on the recent trend toward casual dress in the workplace and working from home. He described how many of his radio broadcasts are actually done from his home studio. He described how, when he first started working from his home, he would do the broadcast in his pajamas. Paul Harvey concluded that this lackadaisical or relaxed approach to his work started to transcend comfort and began to affect his work. He noted that the quality of his broadcast seemed to be slipping. Realizing that his pajama attire was comfortable he concluded that it was, in fact, *too* comfortable and it was affecting the tone and professionalism of his broadcast.

Now, if that type of environmental influence can change the performance level of a consummate professional like Paul Harvey, you certainly realize that environmental circumstances can and will affect how you come across over the phone. Set some easy ground rules for your calls.

First, it is important to dress in such a way that you feel like a professional. If you doubt the true impact of dress and how it makes you feel, and more importantly how you project yourself, make three calls in your pajamas and then three calls in more businesslike attire. Again, mind-set here is very important. Remember, you are the CEO of your own company. How would you dress if you were the CEO of a multi-million dollar company when you were at work? If dress makes you feel more professional while you are making your calls, use this to your advantage.

Second, again remembering that you are the CEO of your business, look at the physical environment in which you are going to place your calls. Do the physical surroundings and set-up make you feel successful, or are you sitting on the edge of the bed with the dog lying at your feet? Now chances are good you will project yourself differently sitting on the edge of your bed versus sitting behind a desk in an office setting with a notepad, pen, and your master list. Your conversations need to be conducted out of the traffic area of the rest of the family, the television needs to be out of range, and kids need to understand that you are working.

Third, know that your conversations will improve with each one that you do. Practice, practice, and then practice some more. Debrief after each one, asking yourself "What worked well about the call? What was missing that would make the next call more effective?" Have a successful mentor listen in to your calls or, better yet, request that she review an hour or so of taped conversations. Give up your right to beat yourself up for not doing the calls perfectly. Declare yourself a novice and be willing to be bad at first until you develop the skills necessary to become more effective with practice and refinement.

Imagine the following scenario. You have never played golf. You go to the driving range at the golf course and get three hours of lessons. You continue your lessons and practice twice a week. You commit to enjoying the learning process, confident that you will improve over time with practice and coaching. In six months, you will be better simply because you have played regularly and worked on your game. In time, you will get good at what you do if you understand that, like any worthwhile skill, you will improve with practice and constructive evaluation. Putting unnecessary pressure on yourself too soon will produce an effect opposite to the one you desire. Relax and have fun. Take the focus off yourself. Give up your need to look good. Focus instead on contributing the awesome gift of your income opportunity to your prospects.

One effective learning strategy is to practice on those prospects you consider not to be your best ones. Commit to having one or two dozen conversations with your grade C prospects before tackling your better ones. Call your great prospects after you have worked out the bugs in your pitch. The process of practice will allow you to get in the right mental state to make the calls. Remember, preparation leads to confidence, which leads to action, which always leads to results.

CHAPTER 12

SHOWING YOUR PLAN PROFESSIONALLY

Successful enrollments will result from showing your company's business plan effectively. To the extent that any networker can create value by showing the power of the plan, those who are open to the possibility will see how they can make money, get free time, and have fulfilling and fun work.

There are a number of subtleties that any associate would do well to master before successfully showing prospects the company's business plan. To make the point, a sports analogy may be helpful. There are a number of sports in which there are important subtleties to the execution of a well-done task. One of them is golf, a game in which size doesn't necessarily matter. A golf swing is really about tying together many subtle details that most people never master. Take golfers who only stand 5′2″. You may see them and think, "How can they possibly hit the ball very far?" But when you watch them, they swing the club so effortlessly and hit the ball 300 yards. If you know anything about a golf swing, you realize that they have their hands exactly in the right place as they bring the club through the ball and then break their wrists at exactly the right time in, what appears to be, a very effortless swing. By creating tremendous club-head speed, they are able to hit the ball extremely hard and cause it to travel a long distance, in spite of their limited height. The professional golfer has mastered the subtle aspects of the swing, thus ensuring success. It's the same thing in baseball. Hank Aaron had a swing in which the dynamics created greater bat speed, causing him to hit more home runs than anyone in history.

A similar thing happens when giving a speech. There are subtleties involved in capturing the attention and interest of the audience. These include timing and knowing when to be forceful and when to be quiet. There's an art involved in touching each person's heart while speaking to them, stirring their emotions, and getting them to see whatever point one is making.

The tasks involved with a network marketing business require the mastering of another unique set of subtleties. For some, the distinctions necessary to be effective in the process of enrollment will come easily; for others, it may take longer to develop. Those who don't understand these subtleties will most likely struggle until they do. Gaining competence in showing the business plan and following through effectively with a prospect will cause one's business to grow. Those wishing to reach the top levels of success in this business and make a lot of money as a result must master the subtleties of these skills for two reasons. First, one must do it well to persuade others to join, and second, one must teach other people how to do it well if they are to duplicate success.

There will also be instances when it does not matter how well you show your business plan. Your prospect may simply be in the looking zone, and the quality of your presentation will not matter as much as it would with a prospect who is sincerely ready for an opportunity. You may have just done the very best presentation of your life, but if your prospect isn't ready for an opportunity and not open to a new possibility, he will not be interested.

So set an expectation, much like you've done with some of the other skills needed for achieving success in this business. You can't show the plan well enough to someone who is not in the looking zone and conversely, you can't show it poorly enough if someone is ready for opportunity. The more you understand the subtleties of what effectively showing the plan is all about, the more people you will persuade who may not have initially been very interested in the idea. It is by enrolling these people that your business will grow most rapidly. Those possessing the enrollment distinctions that cause others to see the value, enroll, and get to work will necessarily need to speak with fewer people to get more involved.

Now, let's return to a discussion about mission, the business that we, as network marketers, are in. Most network marketers who do not understand the subtleties of this business will tell you that their mission is to be able to get prospects to understand the marketing plan. They want prospects to understand how they make money and how much money the prospects can earn. They want prospects to get the details of how the compensation plan pays out. They want prospects to understand the value of the products. If you believe that's your mission, you're probably going to have a difficult time growing a big network marketing business.

There are two things you should have as a mission when you show prospects the business plan. Number one, find out what the prospect wants in life, and number two, create a connection between what it is that they want and the opportunity that you are showing them. This concept is so important, it bears repeating, because this subtlety can be the difference between you making $500 a month or making $50,000 a month. Your mission in showing the plan is not to get your prospects to understand the numbers and all the details of your plan. It doesn't matter how explicit you get and how clear you make it. It doesn't matter if you present it with a PowerPoint, a whiteboard, a flipchart, or a flash presentation on the Internet. Prospects will not remember any of those numbers. They will not remember much of the information you dump upon them. When you are showing someone a business plan, the subtlety that can make you wealthy is understanding that it's not so much about the numbers or details of your plan as it is about *the people you are showing it too!* It's about what *they* want. It's about you having the people skills to get into a conversation with someone you've just met and reach the point where you can ask them things like, "What's important in your life?" "What is it that you are trying to accomplish with all of the work you are doing?" "What are your dreams, goals, and ambitions?" "What are the things that you are willing to get out of your comfort zone and fight for to make life really worthwhile?" "Is there a vision for your life that you'd like to have happen that's not happening right now by doing whatever it is that you are doing?"

If you develop the skills that enable you to find out what someone wants and then help them create a connection between this want and the opportunity that you are offering them, you've won. You will be able to develop a huge network marketing organization, because people will then come into this business not intellectually; they will come into this business emotionally. They will have the desires of their hearts instead of just their heads tied to this business opportunity. If you only tie their heads to a business opportunity, you won't get nearly the results that you will if you tie their hearts to it. Passion comes from the heart, not the head. It is the driving force that will cause your new business partner to do what is inconvenient and often downright uncomfortable to do. When you can successfully tie your new person's passion in with a positive expectation that they will be successful if they follow your lead and do what you say, they're in *and* they're self-motivated!

It really isn't important if your prospect is someone you know or someone you don't know, you simply must get to the point where you can find out what they want. If all you are doing is showing them a business presentation, you will not bring in the type of people that you want in your business. Furthermore, they won't come in the way you want (passionately self-motivated and on fire) unless you develop that methodology.

Now understand this: There is no right way that works for everyone. You've got to develop a personal style that works for you. You've got to go out and practice, experiencing trial and error. In other words, give up your need to do it perfectly at first. You are a novice, learning to be effective as you go. You're probably going to need to do it badly for some time, until you develop your skills. You might do it poorly in the beginning and be terrible with your presentation, but if you keep doing it, you'll get better. Don't worry about showing your plan flawlessly. It's not important to know all of the numbers. It's not important to be perfect in every aspect of your sponsoring presentation. It's important to develop the necessary skill set in showing your business plan to find out what that prospect wants. Get into your prospect's world. Discover what's truly important to them and what's missing in their life. Uncover the discontent and offer a way to fill the void and take away the pain. Only then can you create a connection between what they want and what it is that you have to offer.

Here are some areas to really pay attention to when you are showing the business plan to someone: Don't try to talk them into your opportunity. Have you heard the cliché, "A man or a woman convinced against their will is of the same opinion still"? It holds true in this business. Most people make the mistake of trying to talk someone into the business opportunity rather than finding out what that person wants in life. See, it's usually tougher finding a need than it is to show the plan. Anybody can sit down like a robot and show a plan. That does not take an advanced skill set. That simply takes memorization and being able to regurgitate what you memorized back to another human being. That's dumping information; not building a bond and putting yourself into the other person's world to discover what it is for her that would be truly worth playing for. I like to say something like, "Jane, before I tell you all about our company, products, and business plan, would it be alright if I ask you a few questions to get to know you a bit better so that we could look together to see if there might be a fit for you?" Make a friend, find out what's important and missing in their lives, and contribute your gift by showing them how you can help them get what they want.

Let's turn our attention now to another rule that will support your success in presenting your income opportunity to a prospect: Be brief and concise in showing the plan. When it comes to making a presentation, this is an area where less is more. Some people get going, and they talk for about an hour, an hour and a half, two hours. They just get carried away and keep going, and going, and going, dumping way too much information on the prospect. After about 10 to 15 minutes, particularly if you are not engaging someone in the conversation, the only thing they hear is "blah, blah, blah." You are talking *at* them and they will simply tune you out. The lights may be on, the dogs may be barking, but their eyes are glazed over and nobody is home! Once you go 10 minutes straight without engaging them, asking them questions, and listening to them, they will turn you off. They're thinking about what's for dinner tonight, wondering what time their spouse is going to get home, or what's going on at work. They are just waiting for you to stop talking *at* them. Your amazing presentation doesn't matter unless you are engaging them in inspiring conversation, causing them to want to know more. And that's the skill set necessary to be the master of enrollment in our business.

So how long should you plan on talking? A 15-minute meeting with someone who is ready for opportunity, who understands some of the principles of success, could mean thousands of people in your organization. By developing rapport and making a friend, finding out briefly what is important to your prospect or what is missing in that prospect's life that your opportunity might contribute to, and creating rich value that stimulates the prospect's interest, you will be effectively mastering the subtleties that lead to enrollment success. Contrast this with trying to shove the business opportunity down your prospect's throat. Conversely, a two-hour meeting, during which prospects tell you all about their dreams and desires, can have the exact same result. It's not merely how well you show the plan, it's how well you connect the plan to the desires of their hearts, and whether or not your prospects are ready for opportunity or can be enticed to enter this state.

Here are several questions to reflect on after you show your prospects your business opportunity. How well did you listen? Did you listen to both what was said and to what was left unsaid, between the lines? Who did most of the talking? If you talked for more than half the time, you likely talked *at* your prospect instead of *to* your prospect.

Good listeners listen with more than their ears. They listen with their bodies, they listen with their hands, and they listen with their eyes. Eye contact is extremely important when you are doing business. If you're asking prospects what their goals, dreams, and ambitions are and you're looking out the window watching kids playing baseball instead of looking at the prospects, you aren't listening effectively. Your prospects could be opening up their hearts but they will come away from the interaction thinking that either you're not listening or you simply don't care about hearing them. Listen with more than just your ears with the intention that your prospect truly feels as though she has been heard.

Also, pay attention to what kind of manners you are displaying. For example, if you are in a business presentation and a woman walks in, do you stand up to greet her? Simple things like that illustrate to people the sort of person you are. When making a business presentation, there are many things going on during that meeting that go beyond simply getting the numbers of your business presentation across. You are proving your credibility. You're establishing that you are a professional. You're proving to your prospects that you are a good listener and that you are someone they will want to introduce to the people they know. It's all about coming across as an attractive business partner, one who others will want to work in partnership with and be proud to introduce others to.

Do you pay attention to what is important to your prospects? When you go to someone's home to do a business presentation, look around. By looking at pictures and things in their home, you can get an idea about what interests them. That gives you the opportunity to make some small talk on the way to building up to what it is that is important to them.

Another question to ask yourself when showing someone the business presentation is "Have you set up another appointment?" Remember, the purpose of each appointment is to create enough value so that your prospect will want to schedule another appointment. In other words, did you move the action in a forward direction, thereby ensuring the need for a follow-up session? Did you create an expectation with the prospect about what that next meeting will accomplish? For instance, you may say, "Tom, let me preview for you what's going to happen at our next session. I'm going to ask you the following questions when we get together." When you ask these types of questions or set this up with people, look them directly in the eye and smile. You can tell people almost anything if you smile and have the right attitude. A better way of setting an expectation for the next meeting might be, "Tom, let me preview for you what we're going to talk about when we get into this follow-up session." Tell him, "Are you ready to get started right now, or are there questions you might have that may keep you from becoming a business associate in partnership with me? That's exactly what I'm going to ask you when we get together next time, Tom." That way, you've set that question up so you can ask it without him being surprised by it. It gets him thinking about it beforehand.

Here's another general point to consider about showing the plan. Were you too detailed in your presentation? If you show a business plan and you're slick, you've got all the numbers memorized, you go into great detail about every intricacy of the compensation plan, you know the thing inside out, it just rolls off your tongue, it's a piece of cake. You *can* be *too* good and it just might intimidate your prospect who may think "I can never know all these complicated details and be this slick!" If you know every single number by heart and get into too much detail, you will scare many people away. They will think, "This guy's good, but I can't ever be *that* good, and I don't know if I can really do this business, so I'm not going to get in. It's not that understanding all aspects of your plan and business is bad. You eventually should know every intricacy of your plan, company, and concept pretty well, but there will be time to teach all these details to your business partners eventually. Dumping too much information on your prospects too soon can easily intimidate them. Being too polished and intricate in your presentation is not setting the right example, and you are teaching your new associates from the first meeting. If your prospect thinks they can't be as good as you are, they may not even try at all. Keeping your presentation simple and duplicable, in fact, lets them know they can also succeed in this business.

Another issue in showing the plan involves punctuality. Were you on time to show the plan? It doesn't matter if it's a phone call, a conference call, a meeting with someone at home, or a meeting at a restaurant to show them the business opportunity, being on time speaks volumes about your integrity and reliability. Being punctual is an opportunity for you to express your professionalism by creating a good first impression.

Consider, also: Did they like you? Think of the first time of showing the business opportunity to someone as a first date. Do you remember your first date or your last first date? Remember how you wanted to make such a great impression, because you wanted that person to like you? You wanted to create a positive, memorable experience that would have the person want to see you again. Well, the bottom line is that showing the business plan is exactly like a first date. Your prospect must like you, trust you, and want to get to know you better. They must believe you are or will be successful and if they join you, they can take part in that same success, too. Yes, your business opportunity is amazing, but it is *you* they are buying. The potential of your business or the quality of your products are truly secondary; if they don't like *you*, they are not going to enter into business with you.

Many people need credible supporting documentation in order to feel good about their decision to join you in business. For this reason, it is important to leave quality materials (or a professionally designed web site) to give them more information about your company, product lines, and opportunity. It is much more important for them to be able to review the information after you leave than for them to understand the entire concept while you are presenting it. Remember, you began the process with the mission of finding out what your prospects want while creating a nexus between that want and your business opportunity. You can leave professionally produced literature and audio or video support materials to reinforce the notion that they will be joining the right company with the right products and the right income opportunity. Your follow-up materials will likely reference particular Internet web sites. Perhaps your company offers a web site that can be duplicated that your new distributors can use and personalize to support their business building efforts. Don't just rely on company materials alone to help you with your presentation. Pay attention to independent business sources. Read business magazines and newspapers and stay on top of business articles that reinforce the value of a network marketing business for those wishing to gain control of their financial futures. Look for articles that will support what you are saying in the business presentation you are making. Perhaps you will find articles discussing the high unemployment rate or the lack of real job security in the workplace. Save them and make them available to your prospect. Always be on the look-out for independent information that bolsters your cause. By presenting credible company information that talks about the reputation and integrity of your company and the extraordinary nature of the products, and by combining your package with independent materials from sources that have a great deal of credibility, you will be reinforcing the idea that your prospects are making a wise decision to join your team.

Another strategy that will support your prospects in making their decision involves sharing the opportunity with both the husband and wife or with a couple who will be considering the possibility together. Even if you have a great appointment with one spouse, and he or she is very excited about the opportunity, there is a good chance that, at home, the life partner who didn't hear your presentation will shoot the whole thing down. It happens all the time because both individuals were not enrolled in the idea by someone competent in making the presentation and listening through any objections. No one can sell your opportunity as well as you can. In the perfect world, you want to show the opportunity to a couple at the same time. Unfortunately, this is not always feasible, and there's a great likelihood that most of the time you show the plan, you're going to be making a presentation to one party or the other. If this is the case, simply set up the follow-up meeting with both partners present.

As you make your presentation, intend to plant expectations that will lead your prospects to take on a leadership role sooner rather than later in the business. How you regard your future business partners will likely translate into how they regard themselves in the business. If you interact with them from the start as leaders, they will be more inclined to see themselves that way and do the things that leaders do.

Let's look at the overall picture of a great presentation. You're going to listen, you're going to ask questions, you're going to find out what it is they want with the purpose of being able to create an expectation on their part (or at least the hope, initially) that the things they want really are possible. Set an expectation of leadership by saying the following: "If you understand anything at all about the opportunity I've shown you, you'll understand this concept. It's about duplication. Now, you can duplicate well or you can duplicate poorly. I want to help you duplicate your business well so that you get the best results from the efforts that you put in. I know you're busy, I know you don't have a lot of time to waste, so I'm going to teach you how to be a leader that will inspire others to join you in partnership. In network marketing, we actually get paid to the extent that we are successful in developing leaders. I invite you to declare yourself to be a leader in this business right from the start. If you decide to join our team, this is going to be your business and you're going to own it. I'm going to take you through a period of training that's going to give you phenomenal self-confidence in your ability to make this work successfully. If we can accomplish that with you, you will learn how to do that with other people. Your people will follow your example and do as you do. So, if you want to develop leaders who are capable of building a huge business, it will require for you to be a leader too. Eventually we're going to be developing a business made up of many leaders within your organization. Say you want to travel for 6 or 12 months at a time and see the world. You want your kids to see the things that other kids read about in books. You're going to be able to do that if you establish a base of leadership in your business. However, first, you must become the leader yourself. Doing so will inspire others to step into leadership around you."

Here's another point that's extremely important: In this Internet age, you have the ability to communicate and follow up with someone immediately. Be sure to request your prospect's e-mail address so you can send him a professional follow-up correspondence. Remember, you want to distinguish yourself from the crowd in every possible way that you can. A timely follow-up e-mail that thanks prospects for their interest, summarizes the conversation, and looks forward to the next step leaves an amazing impression of competence and professionalism on the recipient.

Think about the perfect scenario in which you have shared your business opportunity with a new prospect. At the meeting, you are very relaxed, you are dressed appropriately for the occasion, you're on time, you've broken the ice with some small talk, and you've started the conversation in a way that puts your prospect at ease. Soon you will transition to the point where you say something like, "Before I tell you all about our company, products, and opportunity, I'd really like to get to know you a bit better so that we might both look together to see if what we are doing may be a fit for your life. Would it be okay if I ask you a few questions so I can learn more about what's important in your life? Tell me a bit about yourself and the things that you'd like to accomplish in life and if you are accomplishing them to the extent and within the timetable that you would really like to be able to do."

Beginning the conversation in this way will result in your prospect opening up to you, sharing some things about who they are and what sorts of things are important to them. Initially, most of the conversation will involve them talking and you listening. You're leaning forward and nodding your head. You're smiling and you're engaging them with your eyes. They know that you are treating them as though what they want is important. As they share about themselves, ask them to tell you more about different areas of their interest. Ask sincere questions that allow you to better appreciate who they are, what's important to them, and what may be missing in their lives. Next, say something like "Thank you for sharing about yourself. That really helps me to get to know you better and be able to look with you to see how what we do may be a fit for you. Would it be okay for me to give you a brief overview of our opportunity?"

Explain in a few sentences about your company, product lines, and income opportunity, explain the value of residual income, show them how the model of geometric progression works (four who get four who get four who get four works well). Also, explain how your combined efforts (should your prospect decide to join you in partnership) will be to identify and champion four others to be successful so that your new leader can be successful as a result. Answer any questions, leave some very professional materials for them to review, and set up a follow-up meeting 24 to 48 hours after the initial meeting. Set the expectation of what you are going to be asking them when you finally get to the follow-up meeting, and set the expectation that you are looking for them to be a leader—not just someone who will be involved, but someone who is going to develop into an effective, successful leader. Speak about your commitment to their success, if they decide to join you. Say something like "If you decide to join our team, I will commit to working as your partner, training you, coaching you, and showing you *exactly* what it takes to be successful in this business. Then I'll work, hand-in-hand with you to make it happen with a commitment to your success that is equal to your own commitment." You do all of those things and then follow that up with a well written e-mail. By making a professional presentation and following up in a timely manner, you are standing apart from the rest of the crowd.

Here's an example of a potential e-mail you could send to somebody. It doesn't have to be exactly this, but this will give you an idea of an e-mail that is going to make a huge difference to them. Remember, you are on a date, and you are interested in leaving a great impression!

When writing your e-mails, just remember to put yourself in the shoes of the prospect. Imagine getting an e-mail like this and how it would make you feel.

> Tom, thank you for your kind hospitality last evening. It's always a pleasure sharing my passion about our opportunity with good people who have dreams and goals. I sincerely look forward to our next meeting at 2:00 P.M. on Tuesday at your home. Please spend a few moments reviewing the materials that I left with you last evening so that we may make the greatest use of time on Tuesday. Please excuse my optimism, but I will tell you that I am very excited about the potential of working with you. I look forward to our meeting, and I've cleared one hour on my calendar, so I can answer any and all of your questions.
>
> With warm regards,
>
> John

Now wouldn't you feel good if you got something like that in your e-mail in-box? Wouldn't you think *this* is a classy businessperson, someone I'd like to be in business with?

Looking back to the question posed at the beginning of this chapter, has your opinion about what it takes to successfully show the plan changed? Making a presentation isn't about dazzling your prospect with all the compensation plan numbers you can rattle off in a slick presentation full of fancy bells and whistles. It's not about slick, it's about savvy. It's not about perfection, it's about effectiveness. It's not about you, it's about them.

In large part, your effectiveness in doing a presentation will begin with getting someone you've never met to tell you what they want out of life. Or to put it in another way, how do you exercise people skills to the point where you can get someone to open up so that you can find out what they want and then show them what you've got that will help them accomplish those goals?

The answer lies in utilizing the language of permission and maximizing the application of your people skills. You can say almost anything to anybody if you ask permission first. You'll increase your personal effectiveness by learning how to ask questions in a genuine fashion. Don't ask questions solely for question's sake. Ask questions because you are genuinely interested in the person. People know when you are real, and they know when you are faking your interest and manipulating for your own purposes. It's also important to start the conversation with some small talk that can be used to lead into or transition into your presentation. For instance, "So tell me Tom, what do you do for a living? Wow, that's great, how long have you been doing that? Tom, are you still passionate about what you do?" A good transition statement may be, "Do you believe in the diversification of income streams, that is, not putting all of your eggs into one basket?" Typically, people will say yes. "Have you heard of Robert Kiosoki or Robert Allen, financial experts who talk about building multiple income streams?" By using language that's going to facilitate the transition into asking your prospects about the possibility of joining your business, you will set the tone that will likely lead to their agreement regarding the value of what you are offering. Don't struggle with asking the questions that will open your prospect up to exploring things further, just begin with something straightforward like, "Tom, with your permission, I'd like to ask you a very straightforward question. I know we've only known each other for a couple of minutes, but I'm going to share with you a question someone once asked me, and it was one of the most important questions I've ever heard. If you don't want to answer, I have no problem with that, but this question literally changed my life, so with your permission I'm going to ask you the same question." With Tom's permission, you continue, "Great, thanks. Here's my question. Are there dreams, goals, or ambitions that you or your spouse have that are not coming true in the time frame that you would like them to?" Pause, then say, "Look, don't even answer me yet. Here's why I asked that question. When someone asked me that question, it made me stand straight up and look at where I was, it made me look at where I wanted to be, it made me realize the stark difference between those two places. That made me ask myself if what I was doing was going to get me where I wanted to go sooner rather than later. So when someone asked me what was seemingly a pretty intrusive question, I stopped and I thought about it. It was a great question. I still think it's a great question today, Tom. Here's the question again: Do you or your spouse have dreams, goals, and ambitions for your family when it comes to money, time, travel, and freedom that are not happening soon enough for your liking?" Then stop and listen carefully. Usually, Tom's going to open up if you have created the space for him to tell the truth about what his life is all about.

Even if you are talking to people on the phone, the same rules still apply. If possible, strive to do the business presentation in person because there are enormous human dynamics that take place when you are in person, face-to-face with someone. Over the telephone, you cannot see their eyes, you cannot see their emotion, you cannot see them leaning forward, and many of the most important dynamics that go on between human beings cannot as easily happen over the telephone. Nevertheless, the same rules apply, even if you are presenting the business plan over the telephone, and even if you are going to take your prospects to a flash presentation at your web site to get them to understand the business opportunity. However, if all you are doing is showing your prospects a flash presentation about the business opportunity without first walking them through the process of finding out what is important to them or what is missing in their lives, and creating a connection between the two, all you are doing is offering up an intellectual serving of information about a business opportunity. An intellectual serving of information is not going to touch their hearts and inspire them to do the great things that you want the leaders in your organization to do.

Of course, there are always exceptions to every rule, but you must remember, you will always want to maximize your effectiveness in introducing others to your income opportunity. Whatever you do to show your prospects, that's what they've been taught and that's what they're going to duplicate. If all you are doing in presenting the business is taking them to a web or flash presentation, that's all they are going to do with other people. Remember, intellectual understanding will not keep your new distributors motivated and involved at a leadership level. The business of network marketing (like most successful ventures) is fraught with many potential challenges along the path to success. Unless you are emotionally determined to break through whatever barriers cross your path, the intellect alone will not provide sufficient self-motivation.

CHAPTER 13

THE POWER OF GREAT FOLLOW-UP

It's been said by many a successful network marketing leader that the fortune is in the follow-up. All too often, networkers fail to follow up with prospects, thinking that they probably aren't interested anyway. Or, perhaps, they mistakenly wait for the prospect to call them, thinking that they certainly will if they are interested. (This very seldom happens, even with very interested prospects!) Successful networkers share the habit of following up persistently (until you get a yes, a no, or a try-me-later response), consistently (day in and day out), and in a timely manner (scheduled conversations to be conducted soon after the initial prospecting interview).

Let's get into more detail now regarding this all-important follow-up process. Great follow-up starts when you are leaving the prospect. Always move the action in a forward manner by setting up the follow-up appointment at the time that you are making the initial presentation. Take the time to get the prospect's e-mail address and demonstrate what a professional businessperson you are through your actions. Set the expectation about what that follow-up meeting is going to be all about, and share the fact that you are going to talk to them about being a leader. This will better prepare your new prospect to be open to the next step.

So, again, in that first meeting in which you show the business opportunity, you are setting the stage for an effective follow-up appointment. You are either going to sponsor them into your opportunity, so that you can help them achieve their dreams and goals if they see it as a fit for their lives, or you are going to make them a very satisfied customer who enjoys the benefits of your products. You also might receive some great referrals from this prospect, simply by asking for them.

Now, after you've done enough business presentations and follow-ups, you will literally get to the point of realizing there are only about 20 to 30 things that anyone could ever ask about your opportunity. If you will go out and show the business presentation and do follow-ups for about six months straight, you'll realize that you are well prepared to effectively respond to just about any question, concern, or objection that your prospect may have. Occasionally, you'll get a rogue question that is really wild, but as a general rule, you will have heard all the questions and objections after doing presentations for at least six months.

When someone asks you a question about the business, say things like, "That's a great question, let me answer that directly." Or you could say something like, "You know I've had exactly that same question before," or you might reply, "You know what, I bet I hear that question more than I hear any other question." Again, what you're doing is allowing that person to feel comfortable with the fact that they have questions or objections. You welcome all these responses and want them to feel very good about their questions and concerns, but you also want them to feel that you are very confident in being able to answer those questions. Consider that, at the follow-up appointment, you are now on the second date. This person is testing you; they're trying to determine your level of professionalism. They want to know that if they get involved in this business, they can recommend it (and you) to someone who is important to them. They're testing you out a little bit. You're in a proving zone for these people. You must be able to prove your value, your worth, and your ability to support their success. If you've had a successful first date, you will show up promptly for the second date and commit to conducting this appointment professionally as well. Eventually you are going to pop the question: "Tom, I'm so excited about our new relationship. I think you are an exceptional person, and I would like to sponsor you into my network marketing opportunity and work in partnership with you to bring about your success. Are you ready to get started?"

The intention of your two-date process is to be able to pop this question to your prospect. Keep in mind, though, that sometimes the second-appointment follow-up does not yet allow enough time to pop the question. There may have to be another meeting, if your prospect still has questions, concerns, objections, or more due diligence to perform before making a decision. Perhaps, it may serve you both to invite your prospect to listen in on a conference call. You must get to the point where you are able to pop the question, but you also must have the savvy of knowing when to ask it. It's exactly like dating: There's a time and there's not a time. You must develop the instinct about when your prospect is ready to move forward or when your prospect needs more information or a bigger picture.

Effective follow-up is one of the greatest skills that you can develop. However, it's a skill that is fraught with subtleties. It's the mastering of these subtleties that makes a difference between mere participation and making huge money. The critically important skills in network marketing involve the process of making a list, contacting and inviting prospects, showing the business opportunity, following up effectively, starting new associates properly, and developing leaders. Mastering the subtleties of showing the business opportunity and following up will speed your business-building rate dramatically. Remember that your success will be a function of your ability to duplicate what you do effectively; whatever you do with your prospects and new distributors will serve as the example to that new person. Consequently, whether you did it well or terribly, you've just taught them how to do it. So if you do it well, in all likelihood so will they. By duplicating yourself properly, you will be on your way to developing a very substantial network marketing organization.

CHAPTER (14)

STARTING ASSOCIATES CORRECTLY: A RECAP

Your successful network marketing business begins with a dream. Not just any dream, but a dream that excites and motivates you. Before you start on the path toward realizing your dream, remember one thing. Life is not perfect; network marketing is not perfect, and you are not going to have perfect people that come into your business. There is no doubt about that. However, if you start with an intention to bring into reality a big dream, your focus on that dream is going to get you a lot closer to your dream scenario than if you just started with no perfect end result in mind.

Let's review how to go about the process of starting associates correctly by recapping an ideal scenario. Although such a person does not exist, for a moment, imagine the perfect associate within your network marketing business. Imagine that you have actually invested the time to take this person by the hand to train this new business builder properly on all aspects of the business. Correctly, you have created an expectation very early on in your relationship that this associate was going to take on a leadership role in the building of a business. You and your new associate both understand there was going to be a window of time during which you were going to offer training, but eventually that associate was going to take the leadership role in the business. Imagine that this new person or couple, whom you have properly trained, actually makes appointments with success-minded people. Your new associates create an extensive names list, following the process exactly that you taught. They put together a full list of everybody they know and know of, leaving no one off the list. They use list finesse and begin by contacting the success-minded people first, prospecting everyone with a posture that says, "If you are coachable, self-motivated, and willing to follow our proven system that can be duplicated, I'd love to partner with you and champion your success. Although I'd love to work with you, I am not desperately attached to this notion, because I know there are an endless number of people in the world that would welcome the chance to work in partnership with me toward the realization of their dreams." Your new partners role play with you before they get on the phone so they can develop the skills needed to enroll that great potential business-building partner who awaits their invitation. You show the opportunity and business plan to the first of these new people, and your new associates in training are so excited that they say, "Let me do it!" You allow them to do so and they do beautifully in making the presentation. They follow the mission of introducing the opportunity, remembering that there are two important parts to showing the plan. Number one is finding out what the prospect wants, and number two is creating a connection between that want and the opportunity you have for the new prospect. Your new associate does this beautifully with the prospect. Not only do they do that beautifully but they also set up a follow-up meeting that is to occur 48 hours after the initial showing of the business plan. They plant the message of expectation perfectly in the prospect's head. After they walk away from the prospect, they immediately send an incredibly classy e-mail to this potential new team member, confirming the follow-up meeting and telling the new prospect how much they really enjoyed the meeting. In addition, they stress how they are looking forward to sitting down and addressing any questions or concerns the prospect has in order to help that person make a great business decision. Furthermore, imagine that the associates you have trained to do all of these things also conduct successful follow-up appointments. Your associates sit down with their new potential prospects and say, "Look, I'm really excited about the potential of being in business with you. Do you have any questions or concerns that would keep you from getting involved as a business owner and building a business with us? I'd like to answer them right now." The follow-up meetings go incredibly well, and ultimately the associates' prospects and spouses say, "Count us in; we are excited and we understand that this is going to be our business and we look forward to taking full responsibility for our success. We understand that we must take on leadership roles and we know we are going to be in a period of training. We want to learn your success system and build this business by showing many others how to duplicate our success." Then your associates start these new people off in a perfect manner. They actually teach them all about the product line, how to use the products, how to order the products, and so on. They get them started by outlining the steps that make up the team's system that can be duplicated and get them involved in a leadership program. They actually help the new associates build large notification lists and then cull their name list down to identify the success-minded people, the ones they would select to be on the company's board of directors. In other words, your associates do the business just as you taught them, exactly the way that will most likely lead to their great success.

This dream scenario does not need to be a fantasy *if* you put the right dynamics in place. In order to make this dream sequence a reality, you must understand a very important principle about duplication that should be obvious to you. The business skills you show your new partners (such as contacting and following up) are the exact skills they will be learning and teaching. Your example becomes the paradigm you will be creating in the mind of your prospects. The very first thing they learn is whatever they see you do. If you are going to have dream associates in your business, you are going to have to *be* the dream associate *first*.

Here is an extreme example. If you fly over a house in a helicopter and drop leaflets stating, "I've got a great opportunity!" and then wait for the people living in the house to call you, you have just taught them how to contact and follow up. They assume that since *they* got a pamphlet and called, that is how they should go about the process of contacting and following up with others. After all, that is what they saw *you* do so why shouldn't they assume that anything you do in the process is a lesson in what to do. If you are expecting an organization of people who conduct their businesses in a professional manner based on the principles in the program, then you must set that example for them.

Okay, so let's look now at the areas that you need to pay attention to in starting a new business associate. The following paragraphs contain several different areas and the steps needed in each one to start an associate off on the right foot.

First, you will want to teach all about the products. You can have the best leadership in the world, but if that leadership is not using, recommending, and selling products, then no one is going to make any money. Not only will you explain all about the products, their benefits, uses, and what makes them special and desirable, but you will stress the need for each person to become a product of the products as well. You will want to train the new person how to order the products by following your company's ordering and fulfillment process. The best practice is to teach the purchasing agent of the house the ordering process. Traditionally, the purchasing agent tends to be the woman of the house, but always ask to make sure. Do not assume they will just figure it out. Teach them exactly what you want them to do and duplicate by teaching others. Remember the three-step training process. Do it for them, let them do it with your supervision, and then let them do it by themselves. It is the same for each one of these areas. If your company has products or services that represent a certain bonusable volume amount, take the time to stress to your new associates exactly what the concept of volume means within their businesses. If this concept pertains to your company, train your people to understand that all of your products have a volume assigned and what relevance that volume has to them making money in their businesses. It is important that they understand the value and the benefits of aggressive product usage.

The second thing you'll want to train each new person about is how to make product sales. Ultimately, everyone in your business should be making some product sales. Some people new to the business may think, "I'm not going to sell, I'll just get everyone else to sell." Go back to the theory of teaching by example. Your people will follow your lead, and if you are not selling, they will not sell, either. If you create a customer base as a way of showing the business opportunity to people, can you guess what the result will be? All your new associates will move products because you taught them to do so. If you set an example to generate at least 10 customers, and if you have a thousand people in your business who have ten customers each, you'll have 10,000 customers in all. Think of all the volume that this could represent every month. But before this can happen, you must set the example.

The third area of training has to do with the promotional materials that you use to introduce people to your opportunity and the presentation itself. Whether these include videos, brochures, audiocassettes, CDs, web sites, or flash presentations, your new associate must be comfortable presenting these to others. Many in the network marketing world follow a party-plan business model. Many use products as a lead to introduce customers to the business opportunity. That's a perfectly acceptable business model that can be duplicated successfully. Many others lead with the income opportunity and go off in search of prospects interested in earning an income. This, too, is a great business model that can be successfully duplicated.

Teach your new associates about making the phone calls to set up the opportunity presentation. Teach them what to say and what not to say. Explain what the mission of the phone call is. Initially, the mission of the phone call is not to show the business plan. The mission of the phone call is to continue the relationship that already exists or to create a new relationship. The mission of the phone call is typically to either schedule an in-person meeting with someone who lives locally, so you can take the conversation to the next step, or to make the business-plan presentation over the phone (possibly using a three-way call format) for long-distance prospects.

Teach your new associates how to deal with questions and

negative objections. If questions arise on the phone, or any time they are trying to set up a meeting, prepare your people how to respond to those questions or objections. Teach them how to show their plan and the subtleties in showing the plan. Remember to teach that if the person showing the plan is doing most of the talking, they're likely just dumping too much information and failing to get into their prospect's world sufficiently. The person showing the plan should do most of the listening. Teach your new associates how to listen during the presentation of the plan. Teach them how to ask open-ended questions, and very importantly, how to find out what the prospect wants. Once the prospect's wants are established, then you can create a nexus between that want and the opportunity that is being shown to them.

Tell your new associates how to dress for the occasion. Teach them about how to create the right physical environment while making a presentation that lends itself to making an empowered business decision.

After going over how to show the plan, teach your new associates how to do a follow-up and how to create the expectation regarding the next step. Teach your new recruits how to plant the seeds of expectation that will lead their prospects to know that they're going to eventually take responsibility for their business success. Stress the importance of showing the plan to both the husband and wife or other partners when prospecting.

Obviously, when you are starting someone properly, you must teach the principles and importance of the follow-up. First, what's the best timing for the follow-up? Second, what's the best setting for the follow-up? The perfect follow-up is done within 24 to 48 hours after someone has seen the business opportunity. It's easier to support the prospect to take the next step when he is still excited about the opportunity. Train your associates to conduct the follow-up in an environment that lends itself to a good business decision.

Getting associates started properly is certainly an area where more people in network marketing falter. It's an area that absolutely paralyzes people because people typically run *through* a new team member instead of *to* them. In other words, they get someone sponsored, get a couple of names on their list, and prematurely head off to the next person, never slowing down enough to train them properly.

There have been people in network marketing who show fifty, sixty, or seventy plans a month with little results to show from their efforts. Many times, they would be much more effective making fewer presentations each month and using some of that plan-showing time to get their new people started correctly. If you will start 10 people correctly, you will outperform someone who has 200 people started the wrong way. An investment of time can pay huge dividends when it comes to starting someone properly. Train each of your new people on strong foundational principles to give them the best chance of succeeding.

Allow me to share an analogy with you. Imagine a huge forest thick with tall oak trees. You've got a really sharp axe because you've been properly trained by someone who started you off in your business correctly. The only way you are going to knock down this huge forest of trees is with the help of other people who have sharp axes, too. How well you train and get someone started in your business determines how sharp his or her axe will be. The sharper the axe, the more trees it will fell. Now imagine that you started someone correctly in business and they are following the system accurately in all respects. Rather than having to face the task of cutting all the trees down yourself, you and a team of people with sharp axes whom you've trained correctly get to work on the task of clearing the land. Many hands make light work and soon all the trees are leveled and the forest is cleared. You are on the way to making your dreams and the dreams of your partners come true.

Note: Dr. Joe Rubino's *The 7-Step System to Building a $1,000,000 Network Marketing Dynasty* goes into great detail about how to become ultrasuccessful in network marketing by following an effective system that can be duplicated, which consists of the following 7 steps:

1. Develop your vision
2. Create a detailed plan for realizing that vision
3. Master effective prospecting
4. Become an enrollment machine
5. Train others to excel
6. Become more effective through personal development
7. Learn to be a truly inspiring leader

Readers are encouraged to refer to this book for much greater detail about how to implement such an effective system to realize top-level success.

CREATING A LIFE-ACHIEVEMENT PLAN

This chapter is designed to be read in conjunction with the *life achievement plan* that is found in the Appendix of this book. It will guide you through the very simple and powerful process of creating a personal road map to your most precious goals and dreams. Creating a life achievement plan and establishing the personalized strategy that you need to win will take you a total of about two hours. It may be the most important two hours that you spend in your network marketing career. Here is why.

Most people who quit network marketing do so as the result of forgetting the connection between what they want (the dream, goal, or desire that got them to enroll in the first place) and the daily activity of building their business. If you or the people in your organization don't have a clear vision of what you or they are seeking to accomplish through the vehicle of network marketing, it is as though there is a ticking clock with limited time remaining before the inconvenience, rejection, and challenges of building a business outweigh the reasons for originally joining. Those who win in network marketing have a clearly defined written vision that is burned into their hearts about what they want to accomplish, how they are going to accomplish it, and when they are going to accomplish it. By creating a written vision that you read twice daily so that it becomes an expectation of your impending future, you will be paving the travel path to your vision quest.

When you write things down in your own handwriting, a very powerful effect takes place that connects your ideas to your intention. Committing your vision to words creates a subtle but declarative commitment to yourself. In effect, you are making public something that's very personal and important to you.

So, let's look now at how to set a course for your vision quest. Like most network marketers, you probably fly to different cities for corporate or organizational events. When you get ready to book an airline flight, the first and most important piece of information that you need to start the process of securing your ticket is the place you want to fly to. We'll begin this exciting journey of your entrepreneurial vision quest exactly that way. It is usually easy for people to visualize their ultimate destination in life by going through this fun mental exercise. Decide right now how long you want to live. Now, I know that sounds odd, but just bear with me for a minute. Pick any age you want to live to. Do you want to live to be 80, 90, 110? Nobody's going to make fun of you here. Just be bold and pick a number that you really desire, and with that age in mind, subtract one year. Now, visualize yourself at that age. Have you got a picture? How do you look? How do you feel physically? What are you doing? When you get out of bed in the morning, what's on your agenda or do you even have an agenda at all? Who are the people around you? What part of the country do you live in and what does your house look like? What is your lifestyle like, are you humble, extravagant, or traditional? Now think back on your life, sitting there at that ripe old age, looking back on what you have accomplished. What projects and activities are you most proud of? What pinnacles have you climbed? What small quiet efforts have you made, noticed or not, that made a difference in the world or in the lives of others? What people have been the beneficiaries of your commitments? What do people say about you? When they are talking about you and you are not there, what words do they use to characterize you? What adjectives do they use to describe you? What projects have you completed, and what people have you dedicated your life to? On what causes, charities, or organizations have you made an impact? Who are the people that will reflect upon their lives and say that you were the person who gave them the direction, belief, and inspiration to become who they are today? Are you getting the picture? Just start writing. Use adjectives, specific names, and make it colorful and vivid. This is no time to be humble or cautious. For example, you might have written phrases like "I am known as a loving spouse," or "a tremendous provider," or "a person of the highest integrity," or "one who has championed excellence in others." Your complete life-achievement vision statement might be, "I'm a tremendously loving spouse, father, and provider to my family." That's just an example. Be bold about what you want to become in the remaining years of your life.

Now, let's boil this life-achievement vision statement down to a simple phrase or description that many people call a personal-vision statement. I prefer to use the term *battle cry*. This will be a portable statement or a smaller version of the life-achievement vision statement that's easy to remember and easy to reproduce, like a saying on a card, button, or T-shirt. Your battle cry is personal to you, and you'll want to share it with anyone in your life who is dedicated to helping you make it a reality. Your personal battle cry will become your unique call to action, as well as a backdrop for the goals and plans that you will make for your future. It should inspire, motivate, mobilize, and energize you when you speak it. It should reconnect you with a fundamental belief in yourself. It should remind you that life is a splendid, worthwhile adventure when you believe that it is and commit to doing what it takes to make it so. It should bring you to your feet and inspire you to leap over the top of any obstacle that might come along that would otherwise deter you from your efforts. Again, be bold about this. Make your personal battle cry ring. I've heard examples like, "I am an enduring focus," or "I am known as a marketplace icon," or "I embody resiliency, wisdom, and ultimate contribution to others." Determine that if you wind up in a history book for some reason, this statement is how you will be remembered. Mark your legacy with your personal battle cry.

Let's now turn our attention to defining your starting place. In order to chart the shortest and quickest route between two points, you, of course, need to know not only where you are going but where you are starting as well. It is likely that during the creation of your life achievement vision and your personal battle cry, you started to mentally visualize a contrast between where you want to take your life and where your life actually is today.

Let's look at life in eight specific compartments or areas. As I describe each area, rate yourself on a satisfaction scale of 1 to 5. A 1 means that you are completely unsatisfied in that area; there is much room for improvement in that aspect of your life and you are not on track at all to fulfill your life-achievement vision. If you were to shout your battle cry while looking at that area of your life, you would just shake your head in disgust. A 5 means that things couldn't be going better in that area. You have a plan that you're excited about, momentum is building, and you can clearly see your vision becoming a reality in that area. A 5 doesn't mean you're there; it just means you are well on your way, you're right on track, and you're satisfied with your progress at this stage of life.

1. We'll start with a life area that most people can identify with—personal health. In this area, consider how pleased you are when you look in the mirror. Think about your energy level and how easy or hard it is to get out of bed in the morning. Rate your ability to focus and be creative. With respect to your endurance level, do you feel like you have the oomph to follow through and get things done with intent? Think about your diet and exercise habits; are they serving your long-term vision? What about sleep habits? Do you get enough rest and wake up feeling ready to tackle the day?

2. Next, let's look at finances. How do you feel about your current monthly income stream? Is it allowing you to live with choices and make decisions about where money is no object? What about credit debt and other liabilities? Do you have a well-defined plan for your financial future or are you managing money out of your back pocket? Do you feel good about your savings account, and will your investments guarantee a secure retirement? Are you accumulating assets at the pace you require to live a comfortable retirement, free from financial constraints, or are you just barely making ends meet? Will you be able to live your vision without concern for money and without compromising your lifestyle?

3. Now, let's consider how we rate in the area of relationships. Are you able to spend the time you desire with people

who are closest to you? Rate the quality of your family relationships and the relationships you have with people in your workplace and neighborhood. Are you satisfied with the depth of the old, established relationships you maintain and are you establishing sufficient fulfilling, new relationships? Do you have enough friends, partnerships, alliances, and resources to live life fully and make it most enjoyable? What's the overall quality of relationships in your life? Do you feel that most of your relationships are going well without undue strain or conflict? If you had a big birthday bash tomorrow where everyone was invited, how many people would eagerly show up? Do you feel that you have enough satisfying relationships with family and friends? How comfortable are you regarding the depth and reach of your relationships? Do you have strained relationships that sap your energy and bring you sadness or anger upon reflection?

4. The next area we'll define is community. Consider how well you are contributing to the world around you and outside your immediate home or work environment. Are you involved in your local church, youth organization, school, or more broadly in government, nationwide organizations, or charitable causes? To what extent are you making a difference in the lives of others? How great is your reach or influence in your world around you? Is your time spent effectively enough, and is your focus broad enough to leave a legacy? Do you feel good about your circle of influence? Is it expanding or do you feel your potential is really untapped? A rating of 5 means you are satisfied and on track to leave the legacy that you intend. A 1 rating would mean that you feel a big gap between where you are and an acceptable path toward the level of significance you have defined in your life achievement vision.

5. Now let's move on to an area that's sometimes the most neglected of all for some of us—fun and recreation. It's easy

to be so focused on being so busy in every area of life that we forget that recreation, relaxation, reward, and just plain having fun are all part of life too. So, have you had any fun lately? Do you regularly schedule time to recover and regenerate? Do you often take time to have fun exploring and seeing new things? What do you like to do that results in the feeling of completely losing yourself? Do you spend enough time doing the things that really give you enjoyment? Rate yourself on your current level of satisfaction and whether you are able to meet your vision on your current course as it pertains to having enough fun and recreation.

6. An area that is often stepped over while discussing the topic of goal setting is the spiritual aspect of our lives. Most people, at some point in life, realize that their world is influenced by a power much greater than themselves. How do you feel about your relationship or connection with this power? Have you established a connection to a level that is sufficiently satisfying? Do you find time each day to build on that relationship and create greater understanding? Are you satisfied with the people and the organizations in your life that can give you direction and development beyond your own spiritual development as it currently exists?

7. Most people spend the majority of their waking hours on their careers or businesses. Because this is a business book on the subject of network marketing, you probably have some goals here, but think about this. Do you feel like your progress has been in proportion to your focus in this area? Are you satisfied with your overall direction? Are you gratified by the work you do? Are you getting paid what you think you are worth? Are your plans specific and achievable or do you just make it up on a day-to-day basis? How do you feel about the development of your business and career skills? Do you have a desire to become a mentor, manager,

director, executor, entrepreneur, owner, or king of the hill and if so, is your path heading in that direction?

8. Finally, let's look at the category called personal balance. Although many of us may strive to achieve balance in our lives, in reality, total and equal balance among all areas of life is extremely difficult to maintain. For the purpose of completing this exercise, consider defining balance in one of two ways. The first definition literally refers to balance. Rate yourself on whether your balance of focus and attention is on track for you to achieve the things that are most important if you are to honor your key values. Are you on track to say, "I spent my time with the people, the causes, the projects, or the accomplishments that were most important to me?" Another way to define this category is to use it as an additional area that is not otherwise described in our previous analysis. For example, let's say you have an area of interest that occupies much of your time. Perhaps, it's more than a hobby but not really a career. You take it more seriously than you might take a recreational activity. You might have an achievement vision in this area that should play a key role for life to turn out just the way you want it. Or, perhaps you are dedicated to a sports activity or other pursuit, and your achievements will define the difference that you make in the world around you. Any area that you see yourself involved in that doesn't fit in any of the other areas that we have discussed so far would fall into this category called personal balance.

Okay, so now we've identified the eight areas of life, and you've rated your level of current satisfaction in each and whether you are on track to realize your personal life-achievement vision. What would it take to increase your score? If you rated yourself a 2 in a certain area, what needs to improve or be put into place to get that to a 3 or 4? If you scored yourself already at a 3 or 4, what specifically needs to happen to make you certain that you wake up feeling that you are a 5 in terms of confidence and satisfaction? What would it take in each life area to be on pace to become exactly what you wanted?

In case you are wondering, scoring a 5 in all areas of life is absolutely possible. Think about that for a second. Can you imagine waking up each day feeling in complete control of your life and your time? What if, at the end of the day, you felt the tremendous sense of accomplishment and gratification that comes with following your plan to achieve specific worthwhile goals? What would it feel like if, as your head hit the pillow, you could sigh with satisfaction and say, "Today I was a winner and I'm yet one more step down my trail of success and significance?"

Only 5 percent of the population ever takes the time to write their goals down. With this simple exercise alone, you have placed yourself within an elite group. Most of us have been trained to believe that we should strive for a balanced life. Certainly, in an ideal world, it would be terrific to hit all cylinders in all areas of life every single day. Realistically, this is very difficult to do, let alone sustain. *Sometimes, as a result of your focus, it is important to actually get out of balance for a while in order to wind up in balance in the end.* Take Olympic athletes as an example; they put virtually everything on hold for at least four years to set up a perspective of life that will serve them in everything they do going forward. Entrepreneurs can be another good example. They often devote their lazar focus to their businesses so they can build successful companies, retire early, and enjoy the freedom and flexibility of a large residual income.

So with all of that in mind, prioritize each of the 8 areas of life from 1–8 in the order of your desired current focus. What areas of life would yield the greatest result if you put your current focus there? Might this deliberate intention to create something extraordinary even influence all the other areas of life positively?

Let's next look at how to design action items in the incremental steps or pieces on the way to attaining each of the goals you defined. Please understand that your goals are typically not a one-time heave-ho kind of event. Significant goals are usually attained over a period of time and will require several small steps that result in ultimate progress. The key is to write down each step that is critical to the ultimate achievement of the goal.

Many goals will either have a financial and/or a time-allocation component that you will capture as action items. For example, your goals may require extra money or extra time to accelerate their completion. With this in mind, you may also need to add an action item like, "set aside 20 minutes each day to (fill in the blank)," or "schedule a one-hour meeting with (fill in the blank)." Regarding your overall financial goals, you'll want to consider action items that specifically mention money in the finances category. These may require that you adjust those goals after you've defined specific action items for other areas. Also, consider goals in the career, business, or personal-balance sections that would be consistent with generating the resources that might be necessary to support other goals.

After going this far through phase one of your personal-success strategies, you should have a pretty clear idea of what you want, where you are, and a general idea of what it's going to take to make your vision happen. Take a moment to notice how you feel. If you've been bold in the vision and goal-setting process, you'll likely feel a combination of excitement mixed with being overwhelmed!

What typically holds most people back from following through on their greatest intentions is one or more of the following three things. One, they don't have a plan; two, they don't commit to executing the plan; or three, they don't have the necessary support and guidance to navigate the obstacles and challenges that inevitably show up on the way to accomplishing things that they've never done before.

Well, you now have an outline of your plan. Phase two is all about execution. Executing a plan requires setting aside specific time and focus to the specific steps that are defined in the action-planning phase to reach your goals. Decide today that you will make time to put effort into the things that you have previously procrastinated doing. This requires analyzing your commitments and noticing where you have time that can be utilized in a different or more productive manner.

Consider the analogy of a ship's navigator miscalculating the ship's course by a mere degree at the beginning of a trans-Atlantic trip. This could result in the vessel ending up in an entirely different country, far from its intended destination. Let's apply this to your life and business. Are you best utilizing your available time to chart a true course for your most important destination—the realization of your vision? Or, are you just one degree off? Once you determine how much time you have available to meet your business goals and honor other commitments, simply prioritize your actions in order to realize your most important goals. Schedule in as many of the action items as possible that support your progress toward your most critical goals.

Remember, those who achieve great things in network marketing and in life possess habit sets that separate them from the rest of the crowd. By writing out your goals and detailing your written vision, you will distinguish yourself from others who lack these success habits. The choices that you make about how you will manage your commitments and allocate your available time will further set you apart from those who refuse to pay attention to doing what is needed to reach their goals.

If you are reading this book, you probably didn't get into network marketing to achieve average results. You became involved intending to achieve phenomenal results. Such accomplishments are the consequence of a solid foundation of habits consistent with the most successful people. If you will take the time to envision a compelling future and then create a written document that clearly defines it, you will have taken your first necessary steps on the path to manifesting this vision.

By now you have probably realized that attaining the top levels of success in network marketing is certainly an achievable feat. If you are committed to maintaining the proper attitude and a consistent expectation of your impending success, you will be well on your way. Of course, this positive vision must be fueled by developing the skills required to make success happen while taking the actions that align with the results you desire. We invite you to make the decision to be among network marketing's entrepreneurial elite who have realized the extraordinary benefits that our great profession can provide. For those willing to become perpetual students, always learning, growing, duplicating, and teaching, a transformational opportunity marked by personal and financial freedom awaits.

Live long and sponsor.

Appendix: Personal Success Strategy

This section, designed as a follow-up to Chapter 15, will guide you through an exciting, step-by-step process that will result in establishing a powerful foundation and focus, certain to launch you toward a wealthy and successful future! As in any journey, the plans for your personal journey to success must contain three things:

1. Where you want to go—a destination
2. Where you are starting from
3. A plan or road map for how to get to your destination

Phase 1 of your personal success strategy will help you define all three of these components. In Phase 2, you will see an example of how to implement one area of your *personal success strategy* and get a feel for the simple process of defining specific actions and scheduling them into your day. Following completion of this section, you will have the opportunity to meet with a success coach who will offer to support you in bringing your strategy to life with purposed action.*

For now, take your time to walk through this important series of exercises. Keep in mind that developing a personal success strategy is really an ongoing process of discovery, so don't feel that you have to design every detail of your life in one sitting. If you have new insights later, you can always come back and add to your ideas. We have found that walking through

*For information on fee-based personal coaching programs to champion your business and your life, contact Dr. Joe Rubino at DrJRubino@ email.com or John Terhune at jterhune@rainmakermail.com.

this with your coach is especially valuable to bring this process to life. Congratulations on taking the initiative to begin. You are in for an exciting time on your personal journey to success!

PHASE 1

This phase will help you define the three components of your journey to success.

Lifetime-Achievement Vision

Your lifetime-achievement vision will be a one- or two-sentence description of what your life is dedicated to. It will describe your future successes and achievements as vividly as you can see them today. You'll first imagine, and then put into words, a colorful and vibrant mental picture. Your lifetime-achievement vision will express commitment, purpose, and focus. To begin, imagine how old you want to be at the end of your life. What age will that be? 80? 110?

Whatever you believe, write that down: _____.

Now subtract 1 year and write that down: _____.

Now visualize yourself at that age. What will life be like as you see yourself at that age? Who will be sitting around you? Who will be in your life? In looking back on your many years of experiences, what achievements will you cherish most? Of what will you be the most proud? How have you impacted the world around you? In whose lives have you made the most impact? What are people saying about you? What adjectives are people using to describe you and what you have done in life?

Write several short phrases that describe what you are visualizing.

Example:

- Loving spouse/son/daughter/friend
- Very supportive
- Always willing to help
- Tremendous provider
- Role model

_____

_____

_____

_____

Now, put those short phrases into a one- to three-sentence description.

Example:

I am a loving spouse who is very supportive of my family and friends. I have developed a lasting and cherished image as a tremendous provider and someone who is always willing to help others in need. My children and grandchildren consider me their greatest role model and they seek me out for wisdom and direction in making important decisions about life.

_____

_____

_____

_____

Battle Cry

Your battle cry is a short phrase of one to eight words that captures your lifetime-achievement vision. Make a list of some phrases that, when you speak them out loud, produce a mental picture of the lifetime-achievement vision to jump immediately into mind. Your battle cry should give you chills and inspire you to action anytime you read it or write it. Work on it in the space below, keeping in mind that you can come back to it later to refine it. Don't let it slow you from completing the rest of the exercises in the workbook. After you have brainstormed a few choices, you will likely have come up with the perfect one!

Examples:

Winning With Honor!

Inspiring Others to Excel

Living Life on the Edge

Being an Example of Fun to Others

Championing the Oppressed

Financially and Personally Free

If It Isn't Fun, It Doesn't Get Done!

_____

_____

_____

_____

_____

Current Status

Now let's define your starting point. That is, where are you today in relation to the picture you have created with your lifetime-achievement vision? In defining your starting point, it is helpful to compartmentalize life into logical segments or areas of focus. In this exercise we will use eight different areas.

As you think about each area of life, review the trigger questions for each, then rate yourself on a scale of 1 to 5. A score of 5 means that you are completely satisfied with that area as it stands today, and you feel that you are heading directly to fulfillment of your lifetime-achievement vision as it relates to that aspect of life. A 1 means that this particular life area could not be more misdirected, has no momentum, and will not achieve the vision you've outlined. Keep in mind that there may be other questions or issues within each area that you may use personally to measure your progress toward your vision. These questions are used only to get you going.

Physical Health

- How do you feel about the image you see in the mirror?
- Are you satisfied with your diet and exercise habits?
- Do you have good sleep habits?
- Is your endurance and vitality at its optimum level?

Score 1 2 3 4 5

Finances

- Are you satisfied with your current monthly income stream?
- Do you have an adequate debt-elimination and cash-management strategy?
- Do you have an adequate retirement plan?

- Is your asset accumulation plan adequate to meet long-term goals?

Score   1 2 3 4 5

Relationships

- Do you feel you spend enough time with those close to you?
- Do you have enough friends and fans?
- Are you satisfied with your ability to create new relationships?
- Is the quality of most relationships in your life rich and void of conflict?

Score   1 2 3 4 5

Community

- Do you feel you are adequately contributing to the world around you?
- Are you able to fulfill your goals to contribute to causes or groups that you care about outside your family and close friends?
- Is your circle of influence broad enough?
- Are you on track to leave the legacy you intend?

Score   1 2 3 4 5

Fun and Recreation

- Do you have enough fun?
- Do your activities outside work and family satisfy you personally?
- Do you laugh enough?

- Do you feel rested and energized enough to accomplish the goals you set?

Score   1 2 3 4 5

Spiritual

- Do you feel adequate connection with a greater power?
- Do you spend enough time seeking a relationship with this power?
- Are you satisfied with your understanding of where you fit into a bigger plan?
- Are you satisfied with the people and organizations that support your growth in this area?

Score   1 2 3 4 5

Career and Business

- Are you satisfied with your progress and proportion of focus in this area of life?
- Is your career and business focus heading in a satisfying direction?
- Do you feel you are compensated fairly for the amount of work you are doing?
- Are you satisfied with the development of your business or trade skills?

Score   1 2 3 4 5

Personal Balance

- This area is defined by you and may include any compartment of life not defined in the other seven categories.
- What is your general level of satisfaction at it relates to tracking for your lifetime-achievement vision?

- How can you integrate more areas of your life to achieve more by expanding your focus with an intention to have it all?

Score   1 2 3 4 5

Now that you have defined your starting place and the ultimate destination, it's time to set some goals to map the route.

Goal Setting

An easy way to set your goals is to simply ask the question, "What will it take for me to move from the score I gave myself to a higher number?" Of course, if you are a 5 in a particular area, you may only need to set a goal for maintaining the course (unless you are underachieving and playing small). But most of us have room for improvement in most areas so that we feel more confident and productive about our direction and velocity.

As you define your goals, keep in mind the following guidelines. Goals must be:

- Personal
- Achievable
- Clear and concise
- Grounded in time
- Positively phrased
- Honor your values
- A stretch
- Set in the present

In other words:

- Be sure that the goal pertains to actions that you personally can control

- Make sure you believe you can achieve the goal; it should not be pie-in-the-sky
- State your goals very specifically and in measurable terms so that there is no question about whether you have achieved them within a specifically stated time frame
- State them in positive, proactive terminology, not avoiding negative behavior or undesirable outcomes
- Your goals should challenge you to learn and grow as a person
- Although they will occur in the future, state them in present tense, as if you are currently realizing them.

For Example:

- It is January 1, 2010 and I have accumulated $50,000 in savings.

Not

- I want to be rich.

Or

- I currently weigh 180 pounds and have 10 percent body fat.

Not

- I will lose 20 pounds and get in better shape.

Write one or two major goals for each area of life that, when accomplished over the next 12 months, will influence your satisfaction score for that area by at least one point.

Personal Fitness

Example: I currently weigh (weight goal).

Goal 1: _____

Goal 2: _____

Finances

Example: I currently have no credit card debt.

Goal 1: _____

Goal 2: _____

Relationships

Example: My kids consistently come to me for advice.

Goal 1: _____

Goal 2: _____

Community

Example: I am an officer in my homeowner's association.

Goal 1: _____

Goal 2: _____

Fun and Recreation

Example: I am a contributing member of my neighborhood (bowling team, softball team, etc.).

Goal 1: _____

Goal 2: _____

Spiritual

Example: My actions are visibly consistent with my spiritual beliefs.

Goal 1: _____

Goal 2: _____

Career and Business

Example: I am earning $2,000 per month from my new, home-based business.

Goal 1: _____

Goal 2: _____

Personal Balance

You define the name or title of this life area and set appropriate goals.

Goal 1: _____

Goal 2: _____

Now, rate the following life areas in order of priority, from 1 to 8.

___ Personal Fitness

___ Fun and Recreation

___ Finances

___ Spiritual

___ Relationships

___ Career and Business

___ Community

___ Personal Balance

Certainly, in an ideal world, people would feel a sense of balance in all areas of their lives, but sometimes it is important to get temporarily out of balance in order to achieve balance ultimately. Though it may sound funny at first, think about high achievement in any area. Olympic athletes put everything aside for four or more years to prepare for world-class performance and the experience of a lifetime. Entrepreneurs typically sacrifice recreational pursuits and other interests for a time so that they can ultimately have a balanced life complete with control over their own time and no limits on income. Our ultimate goal is to support you to achieve that perfect balance you're after.

As you build your network marketing business, consider the concept of *integration*. By asking yourself the question, How can I have it all? new possibilities will often become apparent, allowing you to work productively, have abundant finances, spend quality time with family and friends, have fun and recreate, stay fit, build relationships, and focus on personal and spiritual development. This will likely require an and-both focus instead of either-or. When we have the intention of integrating the various areas of life, we will often find it is possible to accomplish much more by creatively combining tasks and achieving greater results with such a combined focus.

Now that you've prioritized your life areas, it's time to develop your action items.

Action Items

Now that you have specific targets set for each life area, it's time to break down each one into achievable pieces or action items. Each of your goals will likely take several weeks or months to complete, but to make them attainable, it is important to identify the key steps that will lead to the ultimate goal.

Action items are those incremental steps you will need to take that will be assigned to specific times, days, or weeks on your calendar. Each action item will move you further down the road to ultimate achievement of your goal.

For example, if you have a goal of attaining a new body weight in the coming 12 months, you may need to include the following action items:

- Measure current weight accurately
- Join the health club
- Purchase exercise clothes
- Exercise at the health club for 30 minutes on Mondays, Wednesdays, and Fridays

You may also need to set action items for any financial requirement or time demand that will make the goal attainable. For example, action items for your new weight goal may also include:

- Set alarm 30 minutes earlier
- Lay out workout clothes the evening before each workout session
- Set aside $100 per month for health club and trainer

To get the process started, pick one goal in each life area and define all the action items you can think of necessary to reach the goal. Remember that you can always come back and add or adjust as you gather more information or give new thought to your process.

Keep in mind that you can do this for each life area, or just the ones that you feel are your top priorities for now.

Using the examples from the goal setting area, we've provided a few ideas for you here.

Personal Fitness

Example: Walk 30 minutes 5 days per week.

_____

_____

_____

_____

Finances

Example: Put 10 percent of my gross income toward credit debt.

_____

_____

_____

_____

Relationships

Example: Ask my children or spouse how their day went.

_____

_____

_____

_____

Community

Example: Ask the president of my homeowners association what I can do to help in my neighborhood.

_____

_____

_____

_____

Fun and Recreation

Example: Sign up for the (softball, bowling, etc.) league.

_____

_____

_____

Spiritual

Example: Spend 15 minutes in daily meditation and begin a daily accountability journal.

_____

_____

_____

_____

Career and Business

Example: Hire a business or life coach.

_____

_____

_____

_____

Personal Balance

Example: Focus on integrating as many of the different areas of life into each day.

_____

_____

_____

_____

PHASE 2

Congratulations! So far, you have identified your long-term vision, developed a motivating battle cry to keep the vision in front of you, identified specific goals that will lead to achievement of the vision, prioritized your life areas, and defined action items in alignment with your goals. Now, in order to move this process from paper to pavement, we need to do some scheduling.

Scheduling

Now with priorities set for your immediate focus and action items identified for the next 30 days, you're ready to schedule the action items. Scheduling your activities is essential to goal attainment.

Here's how you will prepare your calendar for the next 30 days:

Step 1: Start by blocking out all of the time you are at work.

Step 2: Block out all the time for family commitments, such as taking the kids to school, coaching Little League, going on a date with your spouse, family time, and so on.

Step 3: Block out all the time dedicated to personal commitments such as church, working out, entertainment, clubs, and so on.

Step 4: Block out all the time for one-time or additional events (doctor's appointment, dance recital, etc.). If you like, you can label the blocked-out times (work, date with spouse, soccer practice, etc.) or highlight each area with a different color marker in your appointment planner.

At this point, you will be able to get a good visual on the amount of time available to work on the life areas that are a priority to you (example: your new business, your personal health, increasing your community activity, etc.).

The examples on the following pages show how to begin blocking out time and scheduling action items.

Sample Calendar

The following example shows what one week of your calendar might look like after you block out all your personal and work-related commitments. Visually, it works best to use a colored pen or marker so that it's easy to see the remaining blank areas. These blank areas show where action items can be scheduled.

	Sunday	Monday	Tuesday
Breakfast			
Morning	church	work	work
Lunch			
Afternoon		work	work
Dinner	dinner	dinner	dinner
Early Evening	Family time		Movie night with kids
Late Evening			

Wednesday	Thursday	Friday	Saturday
	exercise		exercise
church	work	work	Soccer Game with kids
work	work	work	
dinner	dinner	Dinner and show with spouse	dinner
Family time		Restaurant dinner with spouse	
		Show with spouse	

The following example shows what your schedule might look like after you begin scheduling some of your action items.

	Sunday	Monday	Tuesday
Breakfast			
Morning	church	work	work
Lunch	Call mentor, Bill; Set meeting	Lunch meeting with Bill	Make prospect calls
Afternoon	Make prospect list	work	work
Dinner	dinner	dinner	dinner
Early Evening	Family time		Movie night with kids
Late Evening	Attend training call	Make prospect calls	Make prospect calls

Wednesday	Thursday	Friday	Saturday
Breakfast with Tim	exercise		exercise
church	work	work	Soccer Game with kids
Meet with Neil and Bob	Meet with Steve	Hold for potential Follow-up meeting	
work	work	work	
dinner	dinner	Dinner and show with spouse	dinner
prospecting calls	Weekly business calls	Restaurant dinner with spouse	Meet with Sally
prospecting calls	Prospecting calls (time permitting)	Show with spouse	

Now let's apply this process to your goals. Using the calendar below, fill in the dates for the next 30 days in the blank blocks. Next, start blocking out existing priorities as listed previously.

	Sunday	Monday	Tuesday
Breakfast			
Morning			
Lunch			
Afternoon			
Dinner			
Early Evening			
Late Evening			

Wednesday	Thursday	Friday	Saturday

	Sunday	Monday	Tuesday
Breakfast			
Morning			
Lunch			
Afternoon			
Dinner			
Early Evening			
Late Evening			

	Sunday	Monday	Tuesday
Breakfast			
Morning			
Lunch			
Afternoon			
Dinner			
Early Evening			
Late Evening			

Wednesday	Thursday	Friday	Saturday

Wednesday	Thursday	Friday	Saturday

	Sunday	Monday	Tuesday
Breakfast			
Morning			
Lunch			
Afternoon			
Dinner			
Early Evening			
Late Evening			

	Sunday	Monday	Tuesday
Breakfast			
Morning			
Lunch			
Afternoon			
Dinner			
Early Evening			
Late Evening			

Wednesday	Thursday	Friday	Saturday

Wednesday	Thursday	Friday	Saturday

Now take your number 1 life area priority from Phase 1 and, using the 30-day action items from Goal 1 of that life area, ask yourself, "When will I be able to do that particular activity?" and schedule that item on your calendar. You will then ask that same question for each action item listed for Goal 1.

Then repeat for Goal 2 in the same life area. Continue to do this with each of the life areas, following the priorities you set for yourself.

When the month is complete, go back over your calendar and evaluate your priorities and success in completing scheduled items. Ask yourself questions like these:

- Did I achieve my objectives for the month? If not, what was missing?
- Was I able to follow the schedule?
- Are there any items that need to be added as a regular commitment to my monthly calendar?
- Did I make the best use of blocked out time for my primary goal and action items?
- Were there available pockets of time that I might maximize in the coming month?
- How will next month be more productive?

With the information you gather from this month, determine your action items for the next 30 days and then block out your calendar and reschedule the new action items.

Once you do this month after month, you will soon get to the point where you know exactly what actions will be necessary to accomplish your objectives. You will love the feeling that you have when you realize that you know exactly what you need to do to reach all of your life objectives. Remember that it is within your total control just to implement the actions.

THE SECRET TO
GUARANTEED SUCCESS

With this exercise and the examples given, you should now be prepared to execute your personal success strategy. Congratulations! This important process has helped you to paint a long-term picture of life ahead and chart a course to make that picture become reality.

If your engine is revving and you feel you have a lot to do, *great!* But before you get started, there are a couple of other things to think about that could make all the difference in the world in your ability to attain your goals.

Consider the following truths about your goals and the next 12 months.

1. The next 12 months will never be available to you again in life.
2. You will accomplish more if you have the committed support of a professional coach.

Trained success coaches are now ready to help you with any questions that may have come up during your personal-success-strategy process and will offer their ongoing assistance in supporting your accomplishment in what can be the greatest 12 months of your life so far.

We invite you to seriously consider the offer for long-term support through the Center for Personal Reinvention and Rainmaker Consulting coaching programs. With both of these fee-based programs, coaches will help you further clarify all your goals and action items, assist you in analyzing your time, and review your goal achievement habits. They also have access to sophisticated tools, technology, and resources to help you confidently navigate the road to success and analyze your personal characteristics that relate to future success.

Most importantly, coaches will make sure you don't waste time going down the wrong path and will provide you with the quickest, most efficient route to your goals. You will likely find that establishing a coaching relationship with a professional coach will pay for itself many times over by saving you time, energy, and frustration on your way to achieving your long-term objectives.

Visualize this: If you had to take a trip alone to a country you had never visited, you would have a lot of questions and need a lot of information. You would need to make a checklist, find out how you would get there and where you should stay. You would need to know something about the language, food, and the culture. It could be a bit overwhelming and intimidating.

But imagine if you knew someone who had already been to that country. Suppose that person arranged a car to drive you to the airport, made sure you got on the plane, and that you rode first-class, with great meals and your own private movie station and a seat that converted into a comfortable bed. Suppose that when you got off the plane there was someone holding a sign with your name on it, and that he made sure you got to your luxury hotel and had organized your dinner reservations and tours, and that because of this person, you knew you would have the best experience possible.

Now compare the feeling of having to arrange that trip by yourself with the feeling of having someone assist you every step of the way. Without such assistance, you would most likely be anxious, apprehensive, possibly even panicked. If you knew you had the right support, you would be excited, energized, and confident. Having a success coach gives you that confident, I-can-do-anything feeling as you navigate your personal journey to success!

Important: To learn more about how you can hire your own personal success coach, please contact either The Center for Personal Reinvention or Rainmaker Consulting today. We are confident that it will prove to be the most valuable component of this entire program.

We wish you tremendous success and are certain that you are on the way to the life of your dreams!

> Joe Rubino, CEO, The Center for Personal Reinvention
>   http://www.CenterForPersonalReinvention.com
>   DrJRubino@email.com

> John Terhune, CEO, Rainmaker Consulting
>   http://www.rainmakerconsultingservices.com
>   http://www.attitudepump.com
>   jterhune@rainmakermail.com

RECOMMENDED READINGS:
OTHER BOOKS BY DR. JOE RUBINO
AND JOHN TERHUNE

The 7-Step System to Building a Million Dollar Network Marketing Dynasty: How to Achieve Financial Independence through Network Marketing

by Dr. Joe Rubino

This book is perhaps the most comprehensive step-by-step guide ever written on how to build a lasting, multimillion dollar organization. *Success Magazine* called Master Instructor, Dr. Joe Rubino a millionaire maker in their landmark We Create Millionaires cover story because of his ability to pass along the power to achieve top-level success to others. Now you can learn exactly how Dr. Joe built his own dynasty so that you can, too. Follow the 7 detailed steps-to-success blueprint and join the ranks of network marketing's top income earners.

Step 1: Visioning—Establish your reasons for joining and create a compelling vision

Step 2: Planning—Create a master plan that will support you to realize your vision

Step 3: Prospecting—Effective prospecting: Who, where, and how and how many?

Step 4: Enrolling—The power to enroll: How to become an enrollment machine

Step 5: Training—Train like a master instructor: Structures for successful partnerships

Step 6: Personal Development—Grow as fast as your organization does: Create structures for personal excellence

Step 7: Stepping Into Leadership—The keys to developing other self-motivated leaders

The True Entrepreneur
by John Terhune and Michael Hunter

In *The True Entrepreneur*, John Terhune and Michael Hunter create a clear picture of what it takes to be a successful entrepreneur. Denis Waitley has called this book "the definitive work on entrepreneurship of our time." Brian Tracy says that, "If you have ever dreamed of starting your own business, this book will put you onto the fast track to personal and financial success. It gives you a step by step, practical, proven system that you can use immediately to build a profitable business. Get it, read it, apply it in every part of your business life."

www.thetrueentrepreneur.com

The Ultimate Guide to Network Marketing: 37 Top Network Marketing Income-Earners Share Their Most Preciously Guarded Secrets to Building Extreme Wealth
by Dr. Joe Rubino

In *The Ultimate Guide to Network Marketing*, Dr. Joe Rubino presents a wide variety of proven business-building techniques and tactics taken from 37 of the most successful network marketers and trainers in the industry. Together, these 37 experts present a comprehensive resource for the specialized information and strategies that network marketers need to grow their businesses and achieve top-level success.

The three primary elements of successful network marketing are prospecting, following up, and enrolling. Here, you'll find a unique blend of expert opinion and practical advice on how to be more successful at these vital tasks. This invaluable resource lets you explore the many various effective tactics and techniques the contributors used to make their fortunes, so you can pick what works best for you.

Inside, you'll find unbeatable advice on these topics and many more:

- Crafting a winning attitude that attracts others
- Mastering the art of persuasion
- Instant changes that make you more believable when speaking
- Identifying a prospect's most important values
- Simple, valuable skills you should teach your team
- Tactics for convincing skeptical and reluctant prospects
- How to work the "cold" market for prospects
- Seven profitable Internet prospecting tools
- Prospecting at home parties, trade shows, and fairs
- Direct mail prospecting tips
- How to become a great leader

Revealing a world of secrets it would take a lifetime in the industry to amass, *The Ultimate Guide to Network Marketing* is a one-of-a-kind resource that will put you on the inside track to success. Loaded with hard-earned wisdom and essential techniques, it will advise your every step as you build your network marketing business.

Secrets of Building a Million-Dollar Network Marketing Organization From a Guy Who's Been There Done That and Shows You How to Do It Too!

by Dr. Joe Rubino

Learn the keys to success in building your network marketing business, from the man that *Success Magazine* called a "Millionaire Maker" in their cover story.

With this book you will:

- Get the 6 keys that unlock the door to success in network marketing
- Learn how to build your business free from doubt and fear
- Discover how the way you listen has limited your success
- Accomplish your goals in record time by shifting your listening
- Use the Zen of Prospecting to draw people to you like a magnet
- Build rapport and find your prospect's hot buttons instantly
- Pick the perfect prospecting approach for you
- Turn any prospect's objection into the very reason they join
- Identify your most productive prospecting sources
- Win the numbers game of network marketing
- Develop a step-by-step business plan that ensures your future
- Design a Single Daily Action that increases your income 10 times
- Rate yourself as a top sponsor and business partner
- Create a passionate vision that guarantees your success

10 Weeks to Network-Marketing Success: The Secrets to Launching Your Very Own Million-Dollar Organization in a 10-Week Business-Building and Personal-Development Self-Study Course

by Dr. Joe Rubino

Learn the business-building and personal-development secrets that will put you squarely on the path to network-marketing success. *10 Weeks to Network-Marketing Success* is a powerful course that will grow your business with velocity and change your life!

With this course, you will:

- Learn exactly how to set up a powerful 10 week action plan that will propel your business growth
- Learn how to prospect in your most productive niche markets
- Discover your most effective pathways to success
- Learn how to persuasively influence your prospects by listening to contribute value
- Build your business rapidly by making powerful requests
- Discover the secret to acting from your commitments
- Create a powerful life-changing structure for personal development
- See the growth that comes from evaluating your progress on a regular basis
- Learn how listening in a new and powerful way will skyrocket your business
- Uncover the secret to accepting complete responsibility for your business
- Learn how to transform problems into breakthroughs
- Develop the charisma that allows you to instantly connect with others on a heart-to-heart level

- Identify the secrets to stepping into leadership and being the source of your success

The *10 Weeks to Network-Marketing Success* Program contains 10 weekly exercises on 4 CDs or 6 Cassette Tapes plus a 37-page workbook.

The Magic Lantern: A Fable about Leadership, Personal Excellence and Empowerment

by Dr. Joe Rubino

Set in the magical world of Center Earth, inhabited by dwarves, elves, goblins, and wizards, *The Magic Lantern* is a tale of personal development that teaches the keys to success and happiness. This fable examines what it means to take on true leadership while learning to become maximally effective with everyone we meet.

Renowned personal development trainer, coach, and veteran author, Dr. Joe Rubino tells the story of a group of dwarves and their young leader who go off in search of the secrets to a life that works, a life filled with harmony and endless possibilities and void of the regrets and upsets that characterize most people's existence. With a mission to restore peace and harmony to their village in turmoil, the characters overcome the many challenges they encounter along their eventful journey. Through self-discovery, they develop the principles necessary to be the best that they can be as they step into leadership and lives of contribution to others.

The Magic Lantern teaches us:

- The power of forgiveness
- The meaning of responsibility and commitment
- What leadership is really all about

- The magic of belief and positive expectation
- The value of listening as an art
- The secret to mastering one's emotions and actions

It combines the spellbinding storytelling reminiscent of Tolkien's *The Hobbit* with the personal development tools of the great masters.

The Legend of the Light-Bearers: A Fable about Personal Reinvention and Global Transformation

by Dr. Joe Rubino

Is it ever too late for people to take on personal reinvention and transform their lives? Can our planet right itself and reverse centuries of struggle, hatred, and warfare? Are love, peace, and harmony achievable possibilities for the world's people? *The Legend of the Light-Bearers* is a tale about vision, courage, and commitment, set in the magical world of Center Earth. In this much anticipated prequel to Dr. Joe Rubino's internationally best-selling book, *The Magic Lantern: A Fable about Leadership, Personal Excellence and Empowerment*, the process of personal and global transformation is explored within the guise of an enchanting fable. As the action unfolds in the world following the great Earth Changes, this personal development parable explores the nature of hatred and resignation, the secrets to transformation, and the power of anger and the means to overcoming it and replacing it with love. It shows what can happen when people live values-based lives and are guided by their life purposes instead of their destructive moods and their need to dominate others. If ever our world needed a road map to peace and cooperation and our people needed a guide to personal empowerment and happiness, they do now—and this is the book.

Restore Your Magnificence: A Life-Changing Guide to Reclaiming Your Self-Esteem

by Dr. Joe Rubino

Restore Your Magnificence is the definitive guide to re-establishing your self-image. Dr. Rubino takes the reader step-by-step through the same exercises he has used to transform thousands of lives. The easy-to-understand exercises will become a road map to a life of happiness, fulfillment, and self-esteem.

With this book you will:

- Uncover the source of your lack of self-esteem
- Complete the past and stop the downward spiral of self-sabotage
- Replace negative messages with new core beliefs that support your happiness and excellence
- Realize the secret to reclaiming your personal power
- See how you can be strong and authentic; use your vulnerability as a source of power
- Design a new self-image that supports your magnificence
- Realize the power of forgiveness
- Discover the secret to an upset-free life
- Re-establish your worth and reinvent yourself to be your best
- Create a vision of a life of no regrets

NETWORK MARKETING RESOURCES

The Center for Personal Reinvention,
www.CenterForPersonalReinvention.com

Books, CDs, coaching, and courses by Dr. Joe Rubino and Dr. Tom Ventullo to champion your network-marketing business and your life. Free newsletter, articles, and success tips.

Rainmaker Consulting Services, Inc.
www.rainmakerconsultingservices.com

Services range from full consulting services for start-up companies to growth strategies for established companies. Web design, compensation plan design, marketing materials, communication systems, and training systems.

WT Powers, www.wtpowers.com/bonus

Online automation system and lead generation programs with free leads available through this link with any leads order.

Attitude Pump, www.attitudepump.com

The most comprehensive library of five- to ten-minute sessions on all aspects of the development, maintenance, and protection of a great attitude.

Mach2.org, www.mach2.org

Richard Brooke is one of network marketing's premier visionaries. This site contains articles and wisdom to build your business on a solid foundation.

Fortune Now, www.FortuneNow.com

Tom "Big Al" Schreiter's web site. Tom is one of the funniest speakers and an overall great guy with lots of knowledge about how to succeed in network marketing.

Networking Times, www.NetworkingTimes.com

This is the premier print publication in the network marketing industry.

Street Smart Live

For top MLM training, visit www.streetsmartlive.com/bonus for special offers.

Art Jonak's www.MLMplayers.com/bonus

This is a great training site with free offers.

VisualTalkPro, www.buildandshare.com/bonus

You get video conferencing and video e-mail solutions. Free trial and free video e-mails for one year with this link.

Prospecting the Internet with Instant Messaging,
www.successway.com/bonus

This is Max Steingart's best-selling Internet course.

Network Marketing Business Journal, www.NMBJ.com

This is a news publication owned by Keith Laggos. It contains timely news and training articles about the network marketing industry.

Cutting Edge Media, www.mlmleadcenter.com

This site offers lead generation with free leads available through this link with any leads order.

Randy Gage, www.MLMTrainingCentral.com

Randy is one of the foremost trainers in the MLM industry, and his site contains great information.

Brilliant Exchange, www.BrilliantExchange.com

Tim Sales of "Brilliant Compensation" fame's training and resource site.

MLM University, www.MLMU.com

This is Hilton Johnson's site, containing articles, tools, and trainings by a top sales-trainer.

Online Automation, www.ResponsiveLeads.net/bonus

This site offers lead generation with free leads available through this link with any leads order.

Home Business Magazine, www.HomeBusinessMag.com

Focuses on working-from-home articles and resources.

*The Network Marketing Magazine,
www.thenetworkmarketingmagazine.com.*

A great resource spearheaded by John Milton Fogg, to support network marketing success.

The Kick Start Guy, www.kickstartguy.com

Entrepreneur magazine's Romanus Walter offers sound business and work at home advice.

The NetMillionaire Training System, www.netmillionairetraining.com

Entertain your way to success with this fun and exciting Network Marketing Board Game designed to train, sponsor, inspire, and empower network marketers to achieve their dreams.

Dr. Eldon Taylor's www.InnerTalk.com

Harness the power of the subconscious mind.

Len Clements' Market Wave, www.MarketWaveInc.com

Real facts about this industry from a full-time network marketing research and analysis firm serving the network marketing profession for over 15 years.

The MLM Business Planning System

The world-class cash-flow producing custom "PowerLine Master Series Planner" designed to support network marketers to grow their businesses with the most comprehensive planning tools available. Contact pls10@hotmail.com for full details.

Purchasers of this book are entitled to receive more than $2,500 worth of free bonuses to champion their businesses and lives. Please visit http://www.cprsuccess.com/15secrets to receive instructions for claiming your bonuses.

Index

Appearance:
  importance of good, 26,
    28, 51
  of new associates, 149
  when delivering pitch,
    116–117
Associates. *See also* Leaders,
  creating
  commitments to, 47–50
  dreams of, 19–50, 59
  expectations of success
    and, 65–66
  leadership expected of,
    130–131
  perpetual list of, 89
  presentation of business
    plan to, 106–110,
    119–137
  questions to ask of
    potential, 102–103
  review of how to start in
    business, 143–151
  your mission and their
    wants and needs,
    121–124, 132–133
Attitude:
  developing positive, 5–12
  expectations and, 62, 68
  importance of positive, 3–5
  making commitment to
    improve, 43–44

  perpetual list and, 94–98
  toward failure, 16
  when delivering pitch,
    115–116
Audio programs:
  to promote positive
    attitude, 9–10
  recommended, 51, 111,
    202–203

Balance, in personal life:
  action items for, 180
  rating satisfaction with,
    160, 171–172
  setting goals for
    improving, 175–176
"Battle cry," 155–156, 168
Books:
  benefits of reading about
    overcoming adversity,
    15
  benefits of reading about
    positive attitude, 9–10
  recommended, 7, 12, 79,
    98, 111, 112, 151,
    197–204
Brooke, Richard, 50
Business. *See also* Business
  plan
  asking "What business are
    you in?," 71–74

15 Secrets Every Network Marketer Must Know:
Essential Elements and Skills Required to Achieve
6- & 7-Figure Success in Network Marketing

From the Best-selling Author of

The 7-Step System to Building a
$1,000,000 Network Marketing Dynasty:
How to Achieve Financial Independence
through Network Marketing

and

The Ultimate Guide to Network Marketing:
37 Top Network Marketing Income-Earners
Share Their Most Preciously Guarded
Secrets to Building Extreme Wealth

and

Secrets of Building a Million-Dollar
Network Marketing Organization
from a Guy Who's Been There Done That
and Shows You How You Can Do It Too!

Dr. Joe Rubino